THE ESSENTIAL

Vegan Instant Pot®

COOKBOOK

THE ESSENTIAL

Vegan Instant Pot®

COOKBOOK

Fresh and Foolproof PLANT-BASED Recipes
for Your Electric Pressure Cooker

Coco Morante

TEN SPEED PRESS
California | New York

CONTENTS

CHAPTER 5 | Main Dishes and One-Pot Meals

CHAPTER 6 | Vegetable Sides

CHAPTER 7 | Desserts and Beverages

CHAPTER 8 | Basics

Introduction

Whether you are vegan or looking to integrate more meatless meals into your life, the Instant Pot is here to help. This electric, programmable pressure cooker is an incredibly versatile and useful appliance. In this cookbook, you'll learn how to use it to make modern and delicious plant-based recipes that everyone will love. These introductory pages will teach you the basics, and the recipes that follow will provide straightforward, specific instructions to get you pressure cooking right away.

As anyone who has used an Instant Pot can attest, it's an astonishingly convenient, time-saving appliance, light-years ahead of previous generations of stove-top pressure cookers. It's hyperefficient and whisper-quiet when foods are cooking under pressure. There's no need to stand around and tend to an Instant Pot. Once a pressure cooking program begins, you can walk away until a series of beeps tell you the food is ready.

Pressure cookers are great for throwing together one-pot soups and stews and for prepping batches of beans and grains for a busy week ahead. There are some unique advantages for vegans, too. You can make batches of nondairy yogurt, seitan, and sausages from scratch, and even a one-ingredient caramel sauce (page 139) that will change your dessert game for good (if you can stop yourself from eating it all up by the spoonful, that is).

In the seven main chapters of this book, you'll find recipes for every meal of the day, from a wide range of cuisines. There are vegan takes on American-style comfort foods (think mac 'n' cheese, chili and cornbread, and sour cream mashed potatoes), internationally inspired dishes (such as curry, tabbouleh, and cassoulet), and even some seriously impressive desserts, like brownie sundaes and cheeseless cheesecakes.

The Instant Pot is not only versatile, it helps you save money, too. Grocery shopping can be expensive, especially when you're seeking out high-quality organic foods. Prepared foods dominate the supermarket more and more these days, and not only are they expensive, they are often filled with processed ingredients. Going as unprocessed as possible is truly the best way I know to lower a grocery bill and eat healthfully. Cooking with in-season produce, dried beans and grains, and bulk-bin pantry staples costs far less in the long run, and the Instant Pot is a great tool to ease and speed up the preparation of healthful foods.

Whether you're an Instant Pot beginner or just looking for a refresher course, read the next few pages to learn about all of the Instant Pot's buttons, bells, and whistles. A whole world of modern pressure cooking awaits you.

HOW TO USE THE INSTANT POT

When you first take your Instant Pot out of its box, do yourself a favor and open the manual to acquaint yourself with the diagrams of the pot itself, as well as the mechanisms of the lid. This will help you understand how the Instant Pot works so you're able to understand recipes written specifically for the appliance.

Next, join a couple of online Instant Pot groups to get inspired and connect with other cooks. On Facebook, the Instant Pot Community is a lively and active space, great for troubleshooting or last-minute dinner ideas. Instant Pot Recipes is my own Facebook page, where I regularly post my own recipes, as well as those from bloggers and cooking websites. There's even Instant Pot Vegan Recipes, a Facebook page dedicated specifically to plant-based recipes cooked in the Instant Pot. Instagram is quickly catching on to the Instant Pot craze, too—follow the #instantpot and #veganinstantpot tags to see what everybody's cooking, and tag me @cocomorante if you cook one of my recipes. I'd love to follow your kitchen adventures.

The recipes in this book were made in the 6-quart Ultra and DUO Plus Instant Pot models. They're my favorites of the models available, as I find them the easiest to use, with the best lid designs and programmable features. They have a handy notch for resting the lid when the pot is open, and they include a setting for culturing yogurt, which the LUX models do not.

If you're primarily cooking for four people or fewer, you should go with one of the 6-quart models. If you cook in bulk and/or serve a larger crowd on a regular basis, consider sizing up to an 8-quart pot. If you're cooking for only one or are extremely short on counter space, go for one of the 3-quart pots. The recipes in this book are written for the 6-quart pot, and can be scaled up or down as needed to fit whatever size you choose.

No matter which model of Instant Pot you have, the panel on the front has settings for cooking different kinds of foods, adjusting the pot to high or low pressure, regulating the temperature of certain settings, and setting the cooking time. There is also a display that lets you know when the pot is on or off and how much time is left on the program setting once the pot reaches pressure.

You'll select a function key depending on what sort of food you are cooking. In Instant Pot lingo, this translates to pressing a button to select a cooking program, or selecting a function with the universal dial on the Ultra models. For example, you'll select the Soup/Broth function key to cook a soup, the Rice key to steam a pot of rice, and so on. Each pressure-cooking program can be adjusted to high or low pressure, as well as Less, Normal, or More cooking time (shown in minutes on the LED display), with Normal being the default setting. You can also adjust the time up or down manually in any setting with the + (plus) and - (minus) buttons or with the dial, depending on the model. Here's a rundown of all the cooking program buttons.

Instant Pot Settings

Manual/Pressure Cook/Ultra

You can prepare any pressure cooker recipe on the Manual setting. If you're interested in using recipes written for stove-top pressure cookers, this setting is handy, as those recipes can easily be cooked in the

Instant Pot. It opens up a whole world of recipes for you to explore, not just ones meant specifically for the Instant Pot. Stove-top pressure cookers cook faster than the Instant Pot because they operate at slightly higher pressures, so you'll need to increase the cooking time by 15 percent. Depending on the model of Instant Pot you have, you'll use the Adjust or Pressure Level button or the universal dial to toggle between the low pressure and high pressure settings. The Ultra setting is specific to the Ultra models of the Instant Pot. It is a manual setting that you can use to select a non–pressure cooking program with a custom temperature or a custom time.

Soup/Broth

The heat ramps up a little more gently on this setting than on the previous setting, which makes it good for simmering soups and broths. You'll find recipes for low-sodium vegetable broth and mushroom broth in the Basics chapter.

Meat/Stew

This one is self-explanatory. The Less, Normal, and More settings correlate to the doneness of meat in a dish: cooked soft, very soft, or falling apart, respectively. For vegan cooking, you will not likely be making use of this setting.

Bean/Chili

Whether you're cooking a basic pot of beans (page 144), Indian dal, or chili, use this cooking program. Adjust the cooking time to Less for just-done beans, Normal for soft beans, or More for very soft beans. See the chart on page 145 for cooking times for a variety of beans and lentils.

Cake

Use the Less, Normal, and More settings according to the recipe you are making, from delicate sponge cake to dense pound cake to cheesecake.

Egg

This setting is meant for cooking eggs still in the shell. The Less, Normal, and More settings correlate to cooking soft-, medium-, and hard-boiled extra-large eggs. As with the Meat/Stew program, for vegan cooking, you will not likely be making use of this setting.

Sauté

The Instant Pot allows you to simmer, sauté, and sear foods before cooking them under pressure, a feature that adds to its versatility. This is not a pressure setting, and you should never put the locking lid on when you're using it. You can use a tempered glass lid (either the one from Instant Pot or another one that fits snugly) on this setting to sweat vegetables or to make liquids boil faster.

The Sauté setting behaves a little differently from the pressure settings on the Instant Pot in that it doesn't display a countdown when it's on. While the pot is heating, it will display "On," and it will change to "Hot" once it is fully heated. The default Sauté level is Normal or Medium (it's labeled differently depending on your Instant Pot model), and this is the temperature level I use in these recipes, unless indicated otherwise.

When I use the Sauté function in a recipe, I start cooking right away without waiting for the pot to preheat. For instance, I put garlic and oil into the pot immediately after selecting Sauté, so the oil heats up at the same time as the pot. This saves a little time.

Rice

Any type of white rice can be cooked on this setting. The Less, Normal, and More settings will yield just-tender, tender, and soft rice, respectively. The Ultra models have two automatic rice program settings, for low and high pressure. Using low pressure will yield fluffier rice, while high pressure will yield grains that are softer, with a greater tendency to stick together. For full instructions, see Rice (page 146).

Multigrain

The moderate, even heat of the Multigrain setting is perfect for brown rice and other long-cooking grains. The More setting includes a warm 45-minute presoak before an hour of pressure cooking and is well suited to mixtures of sturdy grains and beans.

Steam

The Instant Pot comes with a wire metal steam rack that is used for raising foods off the bottom of the pot for steaming under pressure. You can also use any wire mesh, silicone, or metal steamer basket.

Porridge

Use this setting when making rice porridge, oatmeal, or a porridge made of any beans and/or other grains. Always use the natural release method (see page 6 for more on release methods) when making porridge, and never fill the pot more than half full to avoid a spattered mess. Cooking porridge under pressure is perfectly safe as long as you stick to those guidelines. For a warm, hearty breakfast using this setting, try Toasted Oatmeal Bowls with Almond Cream (page 26).

Slow Cook

The Instant Pot is also designed with a slow-cook function. The Less, Normal, and More settings on the Instant Pot correspond to the Low, Medium, and High settings on a slow cooker, but the heating element in the Instant Pot is a focused source in the bottom of the pot, so the heat distribution is a little different from that of a slow cooker. If you come across a great new slow cooker recipe or have some old favorites that you'd like to make, you can use this setting. When using the Instant Pot for slow cooking (or any non-pressure setting), a tight seal is not required, so you can use an easy-to-clean tempered glass lid (either the one available from Instant Pot or any lid that fits on the pot) rather than the pressure cooker lid.

Yogurt

This setting has two yogurt-related functions: it sterilizes milk on the More setting and then turns the milk into yogurt on the Normal setting. Homemade non-dairy yogurt is easy to make and more economical than store-bought. You can even culture the yogurt right in a glass container inside the pot using my method on page 18. This is my preferred way to make yogurt, since the ingredients go from Instant Pot to fridge with zero cleanup.

Sterilize

The Normal setting sterilizes at about 230°F (110°C), and the More setting sterilizes at about 240°F (115°C). This program can be used for baby bottles, canning jars, or any other heatproof items you want to sterilize.

Operation Keys

These are the buttons that adjust the pressure, cooking time, and, in certain cases, the heat level of whatever cooking program you've selected. Most Instant Pot models have an Adjust button that toggles among the Less, Normal, and More time and heat settings. For pressure settings, it adjusts the time, and for non-pressure settings, including Yogurt, Slow Cook, and Sauté, it adjusts the heat level. The + (plus) and - (minus) buttons adjust the cooking time up and down, respectively.

The DUO60 Plus has a dedicated Pressure button instead of Adjust and/or Pressure buttons, and you press the appropriate function key more than once to toggle among the Less, Normal, and More time and heat settings. The LUX60 model pressure cooks at only High Pressure. It does not have a Low Pressure setting.

The Ultra has a universal dial that allows you to toggle between all of the Instant Pot cooking programs, pressure settings, heat levels, and cooking times, including a highly customizable Ultra setting.

Delay Start

Many Instant Pot models allow you to delay the start of the cooking time for a recipe. You won't find many uses for this function, as you typically won't want to leave perishable foods in the Instant Pot for any length of time before cooking them. The one task I do like this function for is soaking and cooking beans and whole grains. I'll often put beans, water, and salt in the pot in the afternoon or evening; delay the start time for 8 to 12 hours; and then wake up to perfectly cooked beans in the morning.

Mode and Function Indicators

These are the lights that turn on to indicate what mode (Low or High Pressure) or function (or cooking program) is currently selected on the Instant Pot. On Instant Pot models with a keypad interface, all of the function keys and mode indicators have a little white circle that lights up when one is selected. On models with a dial, the selected function is backlit.

Keep Warm/Cancel

This button has two separate functions: it cancels any cooking program and it puts the pot on the Keep Warm setting, similar to the warming setting on a slow cooker. The DUO60, DUO60 Plus, and Ultra models have separate buttons for the Keep Warm and Cancel functions.

The Lid and Releasing Pressure

Now that you know the basic terminology for everything on the front panel of the pot, let's talk about the lid. The lids of the various Instant Pot models (LUX, DUO, Ultra, and SMART) all look slightly different, but they have similar mechanisms. The MAX has a wider range of pressure release modes, including an intermediate setting that allows for a gradual pressure release.

Sealing Ring

The only part of the lid that you'll likely have to replace eventually is the silicone sealing ring, which is seated in a rack inside the perimeter of the lid. It has a life of 6 to 18 months, depending on how frequently you use your Instant Pot. The sealing ring needs to be seated properly in the lid for the pot to come up to pressure, so make sure to replace it securely in the sealing ring rack after you've cleaned it. I keep separate sealing rings for sweet and savory foods because the ring can retain strong odors.

Anti-Block Shield

The little metal cap that fits on the inner part of the exhaust valve on the underside of the lid is the anti-block shield. It helps to keep foamy foods from blocking the valve. It's good practice to remove it and clean it after each use of the pot.

Pressure/Steam Release

The Pressure Release, also called Steam Release on some models, can be set to two positions: Sealing or Venting. When the pot is closed and the Pressure Release is set to Sealing, the pot can come up to pressure. When the cooking program is finished, you can move the Pressure Release to Venting to release the steam from the pot, making it safe to open. And it's okay if the Pressure Release jiggles a bit or seems as if it is not fully secured. It's supposed to feel that way. You can remove it for cleaning as well.

Pressure Releases: Quick, Natural, and Timed Natural

You can release the pressure on the Instant Pot in three different ways.

1. Quick Pressure Release: The moment the cooking program finishes, move the Pressure Release to Venting. This will cause a forceful plume of steam to issue forth, releasing the pressure from the Instant Pot. Use this method for delicate foods that require just a few minutes of cooking, like steamed vegetables.

2. Natural Pressure Release: Rather than moving the Pressure Release, do nothing. Once a cooking program finishes, the pot will gradually lose pressure on its own as it cools. This can take anywhere from a few minutes to 30 minutes or more. That's because the pot retains more or less heat and pressure depending on the volume of food inside. The pot automatically defaults to its Keep Warm setting at the end of a cooking program, and you can leave it for up to 10 hours before it will shut off completely.

3. Timed Natural Pressure Release: I often wait 10 or 15 minutes after the end of a cooking program, then move the Pressure Release to Venting to release a less geyserlike amount of steam from the pot.

Determining Which Release Method to Use

Use the quick pressure release method for:

Steamed Vegetables Release the pressure quickly (immediately after the cooking program ends) when cooking asparagus, broccoli, cauliflower, and any other vegetables you prefer lightly steamed or braised. I'll often set the cooking time to 0 (zero) minutes for these foods, so they cook only for the time it takes for the pot to come up to pressure plus the time required for a quick pressure release. It's my favorite trick for asparagus, in particular, which is so easy to overcook on the stove.

Cooking with Minimal Liquid If you are cooking a recipe with minimal liquid (1 cup or less), the food won't create foam as it cooks, and the pot is less than half full, you can safely use the quick pressure release method before opening the pot immediately after the cooking program ends. The recipe for Smoky Collard Greens and Carrots (page 121) is a great example of this.

Use the natural pressure release method for:

Very Full Pots of Food If you've filled the Instant Pot to its maximum capacity (half or two-thirds full, depending on the type of food you're cooking), the safest way to open the pot after cooking is with a natural pressure release. This prevents messes that can result from food or liquid sputtering out of the pressure release valve.

Foamy Foods Beans, porridge, and cooked fruits such as applesauce, jams, and compotes have a tendency to sputter and spit when a quick release is used. These are all foods that tend to foam up when boiled or otherwise expand when cooked. Although quick release can work with very small batches of these foods, in general, it's safest to let the pressure release naturally, using a timed natural pressure release of at least 10 minutes.

Baked Goods and Cheesecakes Using a timed natural pressure release for at least 10 minutes allows fluffy baked goods and cheesecakes to settle. Releasing the pressure quickly can cause these delicate foods to break apart and may make a mess inside the pot.

Use the timed natural pressure release method for:

Pasta If you're cooking 1 pound or less of dried pasta (or 8 ounces or less in a 3-quart Instant Pot), the best way to get an al dente result is to set the cooking time for half the time recommended on the package, then let the pressure release naturally for 5 minutes before moving the Pressure Release to Venting and releasing the remaining pressure.

Half-Full Pots The time needed for the initial natural release will vary depending on the volume of food in the pot. It's difficult to come up with a hard-and-fast rule for how long you should wait before venting. In recipes where I've stated that you should let the pressure release for "at least" a given amount of time, that means you should wait that long after the cooking program ends before manually venting (a timed natural pressure release), or you can leave the pot to completely release naturally. The amount of time required for a timed natural release varies based on the volume of food in the pot and whether or not it's a food that has a tendency to foam, and whether or not you're trying to make use of the remaining heat.

If you're cooking a half-batch of a recipe that would otherwise require a very long natural release, or if the pot is not filled to capacity, the pot will cool down and lose pressure much faster, and it will be safe to open in far less time than a very full pot. As long as you wait the minimum amount of time, you can open the pot whenever it is convenient. If you've doubled the recipe, though, it is safest to let the pressure fully release naturally.

SLOW COOKER–STYLE CONVENIENCE

The Instant Pot's convenience lies in its ability to not only cook foods fast but also to hold them at temperature on the Keep Warm setting for up to 10 hours, much like a slow cooker. This means you can put the ingredients in the pot in the morning and set the cooking program. When the cooking is complete, the program will automatically switch to the Keep Warm setting, the pressure will release naturally, and you can come home to a piping-hot meal. Soups, chilis, and stews hold up particularly well when left on the Keep Warm setting.

Maximum Fill Levels

No matter what type of pressure cooker you are using, overfilling the pot can result in safety and performance issues, as food can end up clogging up the valve and the pressure release mechanisms in the lid.

Depending on what you are cooking, you can safely fill your Instant Pot halfway or two-thirds full. The inner pot in most models is stamped with half and two-thirds fill lines, so make sure the food doesn't come up past the line.

Fill the pot no more than halfway full for dried beans, grains, pastas, porridges, fruit sauces, and any other foods that can foam up when boiled or that expand when cooked.

Fill the pot no more than two-thirds full for stocks, soups, stews, substantial main dishes, and steamed vegetables.

Pot-in-Pot Cooking and Steam Racks

You may have heard the term "pot-in-pot cooking" from Instant Pot aficionados—it's also referred to sometimes as PIP cooking. This simply means using an additional piece of cookware—whether it's a cake pan, soufflé dish, Pyrex container, stainless steel bowl, or stacked stainless-steel pan (similar to an Indian-style tiffin)—and nesting it inside the inner pot of the Instant Pot.

This method greatly expands the categories of food that you can make in a pressure cooker. Foods that would otherwise scorch on the pot bottom, baked goods such as brownies and cheesecakes, and foods with too little liquid to get up to pressure can be prepared this way. With pot-in-pot cooking, the food is cooked by steam. You put a cup or two of water in the inner pot and the vessel containing the food sits on top of a steam rack.

In this book, I refer to three different kinds of steam racks: wire metal steam rack, tall steam rack, and long-handled silicone steam rack. See the section that follows for more information on each of these.

ESSENTIAL TOOLS AND ACCESSORIES

You can absolutely start cooking in the Instant Pot without buying additional accessories or tools. If you're like me, though, you'll have fun outfitting your kitchen with a few odds and ends that make Instant Pot cooking more convenient and enjoyable. Some of these items will expand your recipe repertoire, allowing you to make many dishes that couldn't otherwise be prepared in a pressure cooker, such as the cheesecakes (pages 132 and 134) and two-dish, one-pot meals like Jackfruit and Black Bean Burritos (page 97). Most of the accessories listed here are available at any well-stocked cookware store or can be purchased online.

Silicone Mini Mitts
Any time I refer to "heat-resistant mitts" in this book, I mean a pair of Instant Pot–brand silicone mini mitts. They protect your hands from steam when you vent the lid, and the thin, flexible silicone allows you to easily grip bowls, pans, and steam racks so you can safely lift them out of the pot.

Extra Inner Pot

If you plan on cooking two Instant Pot dishes in one night or covering the pot and storing it in the fridge, it's nice to have an extra inner pot ready to go. When storing the Instant Pot, I always make sure to leave the inner pot in the housing, in case anyone adds food or liquid to the pot without first checking if the inner pot is in place.

Extra Sealing Rings

The flexible silicone sealing ring that comes with your Instant Pot will eventually wear out and need to be replaced, usually in 6 to 18 months, depending on how often you use your Instant Pot. Instant Pot's online store sells both clear and colored varieties. I like to keep a designated ring for desserts because strong odors can sometimes linger on the silicone. Using colored rings helps me remember which one to use for which purpose.

Tempered Glass Lid

You can purchase a glass lid from Instant Pot or use one from another pot in your kitchen if you happen to have one that fits. I use it most often on the Sauté setting, to quickly bring a liquid to a boil or to sweat vegetables. A glass lid is also useful for the Slow Cook setting.

Blenders (Immersion and Countertop)

Blenders makes quick, low-mess work of blending sauces; pureeing fruits and vegetables; and emulsifying vinaigrettes, mayonnaise, and aioli. I use an immersion blender and a widemouthed pint jar for small batches, and a countertop blender for larger quantities. In lieu of an immersion blender, personal-sized bullet-style blenders and small food processors (with a 4-cup capacity or less) also work well for small batches. With immersion blenders, it's extremely important to remember safety first: be sure to unplug the blender and eject the blade assembly from the motor before cleaning.

Kitchen Tongs

Since everything in this book cooks in a deep pot, tongs are a helpful tool for turning and tossing ingredients. The OXO 12-inch tongs are my favorite: they're made of sturdier metal than most and have a solid, well-made spring.

Sautéing Spatula or Wooden Spoon

The well-loved white spatula is my favorite for sautéing foods in the Instant Pot. It is made by Exoglass from a composite material that is heat resistant up to 430°F. When I sauté vegetables in the Instant Pot, I use this spatula. Its slim profile also makes it great for stirring up large quantities of food without sloshing anything out of the pot. Of course, any wooden cooking spoon will work, too.

Bowls, Pans, and Dishes

There is a wide variety of bowls, pans, and dishes that fit into the 6-quart Instant Pot for pot-in-pot cooking (see page 9). My favorites are my Vollrath-brand 1½-quart stainless-steel bowl (both their thinner and thicker ones work well), the tempered glass Pyrex 7-cup round food storage dish, and a 1½-quart ceramic soufflé dish. I use a 7-inch springform pan for cheesecakes and a 7 by 3-inch round cake pan for cakes and breads. A silicone egg-bite mold is useful for just one thing—egg bites—and you can make a vegan version with chickpea flour (page 33).

Silicone Muffin Pans and Mini Loaf Pans

These small-capacity pans are great for freezing foods, including leftovers, in small portions. Having staples such as broths and sauces frozen in small portions makes for easy meal preparation, as they're quick to thaw. Plus, you can defrost only the quantity you need. Portion the food into silicone pans and freeze until solid. Unmold, transfer to ziplock plastic freezer bags, label the bags with the date and contents, and store the bags in the freezer.

Wire Metal Steam Rack

This is the one accessory that comes with your Instant Pot. In the manual, it is referred to simply as the "steam rack." It has arms that can be used to lift foods in and out of the pot. You can use the rack to steam vegetables and seitan sausages (page 80). Make sure to wear heat-resistant mitts when touching the rack, as it will be hot when you open the pot.

Tall Steam Rack

This kind of rack allows you to cook two things at once. I often use one to hold a bowl of rice and water above a dish that's cooking underneath. (I use a 1½-quart stainless-steel bowl with sloped sides to ensure all the rice is submerged in liquid. This way, the rice always cooks evenly, even amounts as small as ½ cup.) It's a great hack for cooking other grains, too.

There are many brands of tall steam racks available online. Just make sure to purchase one that's 6 inches in diameter and 2¾ to 3 inches tall so that it will stand high enough to use for pot-in-pot cooking.

Long-Handled Silicone Steam Rack

This is great for recipes requiring a soufflé dish, high-sided cake pan, or round heatproof glass container.

I like the silicone steam rack from Instant Pot, as well as the silicone pressure cooker sling made by OXO. Both have handles long enough that you can easily lower and lift a dish into and out of the pot, and they are easy to grip.

If you don't have a long-handled silicone steam rack, you can make a sling out of aluminum foil and use it to lower and lift the dish into and out of the pot. To make an aluminum foil sling, fold a 20-inch-long sheet of aluminum foil in half lengthwise, then in half again, creating a 3-inch-wide strip. Center it underneath the pan, dish, or cooking vessel. Place the wire metal steam rack in the Instant Pot and pour in as much water as the recipe indicates. Firmly grab the ends of the foil strip and use it as a sling to lower the cooking vessel into the pot. Fold the ends of the sling so they fit into the pot. After cooking, use the sling to lift the cooking vessel out of the pot.

Steamer Basket

A wire-mesh, silicone, or expandable metal steamer basket is necessary for steaming vegetables in the Instant Pot. My favorite is a wire-mesh model from the Instant Perrrt brand, as it has sturdily attached, easy-to-grab handles.

Jar Lifters and Jam Funnels

These are especially useful for making yogurt and also for ladling jam into jars.

THE VEGAN PANTRY

Pressure cooking is unique in that it's done in a hermetically sealed environment. A fair amount of liquid is needed for the pot to seal and come up to pressure, and very little moisture evaporates from the food as it cooks. This means that flavors don't concentrate in the same way as they would in a Dutch oven on the stove top. To compensate for this, I keep a few go-to ingredients in my pantry to amp up flavor and absorb moisture. Here are my favorites.

Broth Concentrate and Bouillon

These are incredibly convenient ways to add flavor. When I don't have homemade broth on hand, I like to use the reduced-sodium seasoned vegetable base from Better Than Bouillon, and the vegetarian bouillon cubes from Edward & Sons. To recipes that call for water, I'll often add Better Than Bouillon in a dollop, even though the label recommends reconstituting the concentrate in boiling water before use. When using bouillon cubes, I reconstitute them in boiling water before using.

Cooking Oils and Coconut Products

Any recipes in this book that have a sautéing or searing step require some kind of cooking oil. I most often reach for olive oil, as its flavor is welcome in lots of different cuisines, and the Instant Pot's medium Sauté setting doesn't get so hot that it would cause the oil to break down or smoke. For recipes that require a neutral-flavored oil (such as sauces and dressings), I most often use avocado oil or grapeseed oil.

For high-heat searing or toasting, coconut oil is my first choice due to both its high smoke point and its rich flavor. (If you do not like the flavor of coconut oil, note that there are filtered varieties available that have little to no coconut aroma.) Coconut milk and coconut cream add richness to curries, and sweetened condensed coconut milk makes an amazing caramel sauce (page 139).

Curry Paste and Other Spice Pastes

Red, green, and massaman Thai curry pastes; Korean gochujang; Moroccan harissa—spice pastes are used in many different cuisines, and they add instant flavor. One of my favorite tricks or flavor boosters is to add a spoonful of spice paste along with the cooking liquid (water or broth) when preparing plain rice (page 146), quinoa, or wheat berries. Just check the ingredient label to make sure these spice pastes are vegan. The Aroy-D brand makes my favorite vegan curry pastes.

Dried Fruits and Vegetables

Dehydrated foods soak up excess liquids, so they're a no-brainer in pressure cooker recipes. Add a handful of currants to rice pudding (page 128), and they will draw liquid out of the pudding and plump up as it cools. Dried mushrooms are a great addition to soups and broths, and sun-dried tomatoes enhance pasta dishes.

Grains, Beans, and Lentils

I always keep a few different types of grains on hand, including rice, quinoa, and roasted buckwheat (also called kasha). Oatmeal is a morning staple, which means steel-cut oats are in my pantry at all times. Dried beans are a popular choice in my kitchen, too. I usually have chickpeas on hand for hummus (page 55); black beans, white beans, and split peas for soups; and lentils for Sloppy Joes (page 59) and salads (page 61).

Herbs and Spice Blends

Spice blends are great for perking up pressure-cooked dishes. I use all types in my cooking, from common ones like chili powder and Old Bay, to herbes de Provence, North African *ras el hanout*, Jamaican jerk seasoning, and Ethiopian *berbere*. I love shopping

for spices at natural food stores that sell them in bulk so I can buy only as much as I need. When I want to splurge on truly exceptional spice blends, I purchase them from Spice Hound at farmers' markets in the San Francisco Bay Area; Oaktown Spice Shop in Oakland, California; World Spice Merchants in Seattle; and Penzeys Spices, which has locations throughout the United States. All of these vendors also sell their spices online.

Tomato Paste

This concentrated form of tomatoes adds body and depth of flavor to tomato-based dishes, so if you're using tomatoes (fresh or canned), double up on the flavor by adding a tablespoon of tomato paste as well. Because it can be difficult to get through a can of tomato paste before it goes bad, I like to use the kind that comes in a tube (it keeps a bit longer), or else I freeze my canned tomato paste in 1-tablespoon dollops for later use. The one caveat with tomato paste is that it can cause scorching on the bottom of the Instant Pot, so I'll often add it in a dollop on top of the other ingredients, then stir it in after cooking.

Worcestershire Sauce and Other Strongly Flavored Condiments

These are great when you need an umami flavor bomb to enhance a recipe. They'll improve chilis and stews, making them extra savory. Annie's and Edward & Sons both make excellent vegan Worcestershire sauces. Dijon mustard is another go-to flavor enhancer for me (I prefer the Maille brand), as well as nutritional yeast, soy sauce, tamari, coconut aminos, miso paste, Sriracha, and *sambal oelek*.

Sweeteners

In lieu of white sugar (which can sometimes be processed with bone char), I rely on other sweeteners for vegan cooking. Vegan liquid sweeteners include brown rice syrup, maple syrup, and agave nectar, while turbinado sugar (the most well-known brand is Sugar In The Raw) is a reliably vegan variety of granulated sugar, as is organic cane sugar. It's also possible to find other varieties of granulated vegan sugar— just check the label for a certification. Wholesome Sweeteners makes a variety of vegan-certified sugars.

Thickeners

Since nondairy milk differs from regular milk in its molecular structure, it doesn't thicken in the same way when cultured into yogurt; for this reason, I add a pinch of thickener, such as xanthan gum or arrowroot. I'll also occasionally add a little bit of thickener to sauces for extra body. Use these thickeners judiciously—adding too much will give a bouncy, overly thickened result.

Egg Replacer Powder

Egg replacers are indispensable for baked goods— often, you can convert nonvegan recipes easily by swapping in egg replacer and nondairy milk. My favorite is Bob's Red Mill Gluten-Free Vegan Egg Replacer. It's the least expensive of any brand I've found, and it works great. I don't always use it as directed—sometimes I'll add it straight to the liquid ingredients in a recipe rather than mixing it with water first.

CHAPTER 1

Breakfast

Vegan Yogurt

MAKES 4 CUPS

1 quart unsweetened nondairy milk (soy, almond, cashew, or coconut)

¼ teaspoon arrowroot

¼ teaspoon xanthan gum

2 tablespoons agave nectar

2 tablespoons nondairy yogurt with active live cultures, at room temperature

Yogurt is the basis for many sweet breakfasts. It's both easy and economical to make it in the Instant Pot, using the Yogurt setting to heat and culture any unsweetened nondairy milk in two simple steps. Sprinkled with granola and fruit, layered in a parfait, or blended into smoothies, it's a staple I always have on hand.

My favorite milks to use for yogurt are soy, almond, cashew, and coconut. They all culture well and have a gently tangy flavor after 8 hours of culturing. You can culture your yogurt even longer (up to 12 hours) if you like it really tangy. Small amounts of arrowroot and xanthan gum stabilize and thicken the yogurt, so you'll get a good result whether you start out with a very rich, thick milk or a more watery one.

For your starter culture, you can use a spoonful of store-bought nondairy yogurt or a dehydrated yogurt culture. I generally go with a store-bought, single-serving cup of yogurt—it's still less expensive than buying a quart of yogurt and much easier to find than dehydrated, vegan yogurt starter cultures.

Whatever variety of yogurt you use for your starter, just make sure it's plain (a little added sweetener is fine) and that it contains active live cultures. Oh, and make sure you like the taste of the starter yogurt, since that flavor will be imparted to the whole batch. Some nondairy yogurts are very mild, while others can be very tangy or even a little fizzy (I've mostly noticed this with coconut varieties).

The quantities in the following recipe can be halved for a smaller (2-cup) batch of yogurt, or doubled for a larger (8-cup) batch.

Add the nondairy milk, arrowroot, xanthan gum, and agave nectar to the Instant Pot and whisk to combine. Do not cover the pot. Select the **Yogurt** program and adjust it to its high setting.

When the cooking program ends, wearing heat-resistant mitts, lift the inner pot out of the Instant Pot housing and place it on a trivet. Let the milk mixture cool in the pot until it reaches 110°F to 115°F. Once the milk has cooled, add the nondairy yogurt and whisk to combine.

Ladle or pour the mixture into two widemouthed pint jars and cover the jars with their lids. Rinse out the pot and return it to the housing.

Add 1 cup water to the pot and place the wire metal steam rack inside. Place the jars on the steam rack. Secure the lid and set the Pressure Release to **Venting**. Select the **Yogurt** program once more, this time adjusting it to its normal setting. Leave the time at the setting's default 8 hours for a mildly tangy yogurt, increase to 10 hours for a tangier yogurt, or set to12 hours for a very tangy yogurt.

When the cooking program ends, transfer the jars of yogurt to the refrigerator. Let chill for at least 8 hours before using. The yogurt will keep, refrigerated, for up to 1 week.

Coconut Yogurt Parfaits
with Mango Ginger Jam

Layer oven-baked granola, a ginger-spiked jam, coconut milk yogurt, and fresh berries for a beautiful parfait full of textural contrasts.

To make the granola: Preheat the oven to 300°F. Line a baking sheet with parchment paper or a silicone baking mat. In a mixing bowl, combine the oats and coconut.

In a small saucepan over medium-low heat, heat the agave and coconut oil just until the coconut oil melts and the mixture begins to simmer, about 4 minutes. Turn off the heat and stir in the vanilla and salt. Pour the agave and coconut oil mixture over the oat mixture and stir so that everything is evenly coated.

Use a silicone spatula to transfer the mixture to the prepared baking sheet, spreading it out in an even layer. Bake for 30 to 35 minutes, stirring every 10 minutes, until the granola is golden brown. Let the granola cool to room temperature, then transfer to an airtight container and store for up to 2 weeks.

To make the jam: Add the mango, ginger, water, and lemon juice to the Instant Pot. Cover with the glass lid, select the **Sauté** setting, and cook for about 5 minutes, until the liquid is boiling rapidly.

Uncover the pot and stir in the sugar. Return to a boil, uncovered, and cook for another 5 minutes, stirring continuously, until the mixture thickens and begins to come away from the pot bottom when stirred. Press the **Cancel** button to turn off the pot. Wearing heat-resistant mitts, lift out the inner pot. Use an immersion blender to puree the jam until smooth, tilting the pot so that the blender head is fully submerged. Transfer the jam to an airtight container or containers and let cool to room temperature. Tightly cover and refrigerate. It will keep, refrigerated, for up to 2 months.

To serve, spoon ¼ cup of the yogurt into each of four jam jars or drinking glasses, followed by 1 tablespoon jam, ¼ cup blueberries, and 2 tablespoons granola. Repeat the layers, then serve immediately.

SERVES 4 (WITH LEFTOVER GRANOLA AND JAM)

GRANOLA

3 cups old-fashioned oats

1½ cups unsweetened coconut flakes

⅓ cup agave nectar or brown rice syrup

⅓ cup coconut oil

1 teaspoon vanilla extract

½ teaspoon fine sea salt

JAM

3 cups finely chopped mango or 16 ounces frozen mango chunks, thawed and finely chopped

1-inch knob fresh ginger, peeled and finely grated

2 tablespoons fresh lemon juice

¼ cup water

¾ cup turbinado or organic cane sugar

TO SERVE

2 cups yogurt made with coconut milk (page 18)

1 pint blueberries

Three Smoothies

EACH MAKES
1 LARGE (22-OUNCE)
SMOOTHIE

Once you've cultured a batch of yogurt, a world of creamy, satisfying smoothies is within reach. I'll often make one of these in the morning, drink half, and pour the rest into an insulated thermos for an afternoon treat on the go. For a more celebratory morning meal, you can go full-Instagram and build a beautiful smoothie bowl with your toppings of choice.

———————————

To make any of these three smoothies, place all of the ingredients in a blender in the order listed. Blend at high speed for about 45 seconds, until smooth. Add more nondairy milk if needed.

NOTE

To create a smoothie bowl, pour your smoothie into a bowl and sprinkle on your toppings of choice. Here are a few options to get you started.

Sliced fresh fruit and berries

Chopped nuts and coconut flakes

Puffed grains and cereals

Granola and muesli

Chia and hemp seeds

Chopped dark chocolate and mochi

Agave nectar and maple syrup

Cocoa powder and cinnamon

PINEAPPLE SUNSHINE

A spoonful of sunny yellow turmeric perks up this pineapple treat. Feel free to halve the spices for a milder drink.

1½ cups frozen pineapple chunks

1 cup nondairy yogurt (page 18)

½ cup unsweetened nondairy milk, plus more as needed

2 teaspoons agave nectar

1 teaspoon ground turmeric

½ teaspoon ground ginger

BERRY VANILLA

This one is my favorite post-workout treat. It's sweet and satisfying, and the hint of vanilla gives it an indulgent dessert vibe.

1½ cups mixed frozen berries

1 cup nondairy yogurt (page 18)

½ cup unsweetened nondairy milk, plus more as needed

2 teaspoons agave nectar

½ teaspoon vanilla extract

GREEN MONSTER

Get your greens at the start of the day, or as an afternoon pick-me-up. For a less sweet smoothie, you can sub an avocado for the mango.

1 medium banana, broken into 1-inch pieces (use frozen bananas for a thicker smoothie)

¾ cup frozen mango chunks

2 loosely packed cups (2 ounces) baby spinach

1 cup nondairy yogurt (page 18)

½ cup unsweetened nondairy milk, plus more as needed

Steel-Cut PBJ Oatmeal with Raspberry Chia Jam

PBJ sandwiches were one of my favorite foods growing up. I still love that flavor combination to this day, even in oatmeal form. Peanut butter is stirred into steel-cut oats, making them extra creamy, and a sprinkle of chopped peanuts on top adds a little crunch. The jam is a no-cook affair—it's thickened with chia seeds, and you can make it with frozen raspberries year-round.

To make the jam: In a bowl, combine the thawed raspberries, agave, chia seeds, and salt. Stir for about 1 minute, until the raspberries are mostly broken up, the agave nectar is dissolved, and the chia seeds are distributed evenly throughout. Cover and transfer to the refrigerator to firm up for at least 2 hours, or up to overnight. The jam will keep in an airtight container, refrigerated, for up to 1 week. Stir once more before serving.

To make the oatmeal: Select the **Sauté** setting on the Instant Pot, add the coconut oil, and melt. Add the oats and cook, stirring often, for about 5 minutes, until the oats are aromatic and lightly toasted. Stir in the water, using a wooden spoon to nudge any browned bits from the bottom of the pot, and making sure all of the oats are submerged in the liquid.

Secure the lid and set the Pressure Release to **Sealing**. Press the **Cancel** button to reset the cooking program. Then select the **Porridge** setting and set the cooking time for 12 minutes at high pressure. (The pot will take about 10 minutes to come up to pressure before the cooking program begins.)

When the cooking program ends, let the pressure release naturally for 10 minutes, then move the Pressure Release to **Venting** to release any remaining steam. Open the pot and stir in the peanut butter, as well as any liquid sitting on top of the oatmeal.

To serve, ladle the oatmeal into bowls and serve with a dollop of jam swirled in and the chopped peanuts sprinkled on top.

SERVES 4 TO 6

JAM

1 (12-ounce) bag frozen raspberries, thawed in the fridge overnight

¼ cup agave nectar or brown rice syrup

1 tablespoon chia seeds

1 pinch of fine sea salt

OATMEAL

2 tablespoons coconut oil

1½ cups steel-cut oats

4½ cups water

¼ cup smooth natural peanut butter

½ cup roasted salted peanuts, chopped

NOTE

The oatmeal will thicken as it sits. For a looser texture, stir in a splash of nondairy milk, as needed.

Toasted Oatmeal Bowls with Almond Cream

SERVES 4

OATMEAL

2 tablespoons coconut oil

2 cups old-fashioned oats

5 cups water

¾ teaspoon ground cinnamon

½ teaspoon fine sea salt

TO SERVE

Almond Cream (recipe follows)

2 bananas, sliced into rounds

1 cup fresh blackberries

¼ cup toasted sliced almonds

Ground cinnamon for dusting

NOTE

I learned a trick from Kath of the blog *Kath Eats* ages ago that I just love—for sweeter oatmeal, you can thinly slice a banana, then vigorously whisk it into the cooked oatmeal. Try it out for an extra-fluffy, flavorful bowl.

A bowl of old-fashioned oats gets a toasty twist when you sauté the oats in coconut oil first. The oatmeal comes out extra creamy, with more depth of flavor than oats cooked in water alone. The sweet, nutty almond cream topping is addictive—you'll want to pour it on pancakes and waffles, too.

To make the oatmeal: Select the **Sauté** setting on the Instant Pot, add the coconut oil, and melt. Add the oats and cook, stirring often, for about 5 minutes, until the oats are aromatic and lightly toasted. Stir in the water, cinnamon, and salt, making sure all of the oats are submerged in the liquid.

Secure the lid and set the Pressure Release to **Sealing**. Press the **Cancel** button to reset the cooking program. Then select the **Manual**, **Pressure Cook**, or **Porridge** setting and set the cooking time for 3 minutes at high pressure. (The pot will take about 10 minutes to come up to pressure before the cooking program begins.)

When the cooking program ends, let the pressure release naturally for 15 minutes, then move the Pressure Release to **Venting** to release any remaining steam. Open the pot and stir the oatmeal, making sure to scrape along the bottom. (It will look like there is extra liquid when you open the pot, but the liquid will absorb into the oatmeal immediately when stirred.)

To serve, ladle the oatmeal into bowls and pour some of the almond cream on top. Add the bananas, berries, almonds, and a sprinkle of cinnamon, and serve.

ALMOND CREAM

MAKES ABOUT ¾ CUP

⅓ cup almond milk, at room temperature

⅓ cup almond butter, at room temperature

2 tablespoons agave nectar

½ teaspoon vanilla extract

In a widemouthed 1-pint jar, combine the almond milk, almond butter, agave nectar, and vanilla. Lower an immersion blender into the jar, so the head is fully submerged, and blend until smooth. The almond cream will keep in an airtight container, refrigerated, for up to 1 week.

NOTE

For extra convenience, it's easy to freeze and reheat oatmeal.

To freeze, let the oatmeal cool to room temperature, then scoop ½-cup portions into the wells of a silicone muffin pan and slip the pan into the freezer. When the portions have frozen solid, about 4 hours, pop them out of the muffin pan, put in ziplock freezer bags, and return to the freezer. Store for up to 6 months.

To reheat, microwave two of the ½-cup portions in a bowl for two minutes, stir in a splash of non-dairy milk, then microwave for one more minute, until piping hot.

Savory Multigrain Porridge

SERVES 4

5 cups water

½ cup short- or medium-grain white rice

½ cup whole-grain multigrain blend

1-inch knob ginger, peeled and cut into ¼-inch-thick slices

1 green onion, white and tender green parts, thinly sliced

Soy sauce, tamari, or coconut aminos; toasted sesame oil; and/or sambal oelek or Sriracha for serving

NOTES

In most Asian grocery stores, you can find multigrain blends near the bags of basic white and brown rice. They can contain many different varieties of grains such as rice, barley, oats, millet, and sometimes smaller beans and seeds as well. Use any brand you like in this savory porridge, or mix up your own blend from whatever whole grains are in your pantry.

Using water as the cooking liquid makes this porridge very versatile—you can top it with anything you like. To bump up the savory flavor, substitute low-sodium vegetable broth (page 152) for some or all of the water.

Whether you call it porridge, *jook*, or congee, this simple breakfast is popular in many Asian cuisines. I like to bolster the basic white rice with a multigrain blend for some extra texture and nutrition. You can top this porridge with any savory flavorings you like—my favorites are sliced green onion, soy sauce, toasted sesame oil, and chili paste. Fried garlic chips, kimchi, and furikake seaweed are good, too.

———————

Add the water, rice, multigrain blend, and ginger to the Instant Pot. Secure the lid and set the Pressure Release to **Sealing**. Select the **Manual, Pressure Cook,** or **Porridge** setting and set the cooking time for 30 minutes at high pressure. (The pot will take about 15 minutes to come up to pressure before the cooking program begins.)

When the cooking program ends, let the pressure release naturally for 25 minutes, then move the Pressure Release to **Venting** to release any remaining steam. Open the pot and stir the porridge. It will be quite thin at first but will thicken up as it sits. Remove and discard the ginger slices, then let the porridge stand and thicken for 5 minutes.

Ladle into bowls and sprinkle with the green onion. Serve with soy sauce, sesame oil, and sambal oelek on the side.

Breakfast Tacos
with Pinto Beans and Tofu

This recipe was inspired by the breakfast tacos at Torchy's Tacos in Austin, Texas. Piled high with Tex-Mex toppings, they're a belly-filling breakfast that begs to be veganized. Tofu is crumbled and cooked with lots of vegetables and spices to create a flavorful, protein-filled base. It'll stay warm in the Instant Pot while everybody eats their first round of tacos, so you can have piping-hot seconds, too.

Select the **Sauté** setting on the Instant Pot, add the oil and garlic, and heat for about 2 minutes, until the garlic is bubbling. Add the onion, bell pepper, jalapeños, and salt. Sauté for about 4 minutes, until the onion softens. Add the chili powder, cumin, pepper, turmeric, and oregano and sauté for 1 minute more. Stir in the broth, using a wooden spoon to nudge loose any browned bits from the bottom of the pot. Stir in the tofu and beans, then pour the tomatoes and their liquid on top. Do not stir.

Secure the lid and set the Pressure Release to **Sealing**. Press the **Cancel** button to reset the cooking program. Then select the **Manual** or **Pressure Cook** setting and set the cooking time for 10 minutes at high pressure. (The pot will take about 15 minutes to come up to pressure before the cooking program begins.)

When the cooking program ends, perform a quick pressure release by moving the Pressure Release to **Venting**. Open the pot, add the nutritional yeast, and stir to combine. At this point, you can serve right away, or you can thicken the tofu mixture.

To thicken, press the **Cancel** button to reset the cooking program. Then select the **Sauté** setting. Bring the tofu mixture to a simmer and cook, stirring occasionally, for 8 to 10 minutes, until thickened. Press the **Cancel** button to turn off the pot.

To serve, spoon the mixture onto the warmed tortillas. Top with avocado and cilantro and serve right away with hot sauce.

SERVES 4 TO 6

2 tablespoons extra-virgin olive oil

3 cloves garlic, minced

1 yellow onion, diced

1 red, orange, or yellow bell pepper, seeded and diced

2 jalapeño chiles, seeded and diced

½ teaspoon fine sea salt

1 tablespoon chili powder

1 teaspoon ground cumin

½ teaspoon freshly ground black pepper

½ teaspoon ground turmeric

½ teaspoon dried oregano

1 cup low-sodium vegetable broth (page 152)

1 (14-ounce) block firm tofu, drained and crumbled

1½ cups cooked pinto beans (page 144), or 1 (15-ounce) can beans, rinsed and drained

1 (14½-ounce) can fire-roasted diced tomatoes

¼ cup nutritional yeast

12 warmed corn tortillas

Sliced avocado, chopped fresh cilantro, and hot sauce (such as Cholula or Tapatio) for serving

Ful Mudammas

SERVES 4

3 tablespoons extra-virgin olive oil

1 yellow onion, diced

1 cup low-sodium vegetable broth (page 152)

2 (15-ounce) cans fava beans, chickpeas, or pinto beans, rinsed and drained

1 (14½-ounce) can diced tomatoes

2 cloves garlic, minced

2 tablespoons fresh lemon juice

½ teaspoon ground cumin

Fine sea salt

2 tablespoons chopped fresh flat-leaf parsley

½ cup sliced red onion

4 radishes, sliced

½ cup cherry tomatoes, quartered

Tahini or extra-virgin olive oil for drizzling

4 rounds whole-wheat pita bread

Use a couple cans of fava beans (or substitute a can of chickpeas or pinto beans) for this savory Egyptian breakfast dish. Traditional recipes run the gamut in preparation—you can simply heat the beans on their own, or, for more flavor, add vegetables and seasonings. I like to brown and sauté an onion before adding the beans, then top the finished dish with fresh vegetables for some contrast and crunch. Serve with wedges of whole-wheat pita bread (the fluffiest you can find) for scooping.

———————————

Select the **Sauté** setting on the Instant Pot, add 2 tablespoons of the oil, and heat for 2 minutes. Add the onion and sauté for 8 minutes, until it's beginning to brown and caramelize around the edges. Stir in the broth, using a wooden spoon to nudge loose any browned bits from the bottom of the pot. Stir in the fava beans. Add the tomatoes and their liquid on top, but do not stir them in.

Secure the lid and set the Pressure Release to **Sealing**. Press the **Cancel** button to reset the cooking program. Then select the **Manual**, **Pressure Cook**, or **Bean/Chili** setting and set the cooking time for 15 minutes at high pressure. (The pot will take about 10 minutes to come up to pressure before the cooking program begins.)

While the beans are cooking, in a small bowl, combine the garlic and lemon juice.

When the cooking program ends, let the pressure release naturally for 10 minutes, then move the Pressure Release to **Venting** to release any remaining steam. Open the pot and stir in the remaining 1 tablespoon oil, the lemon juice/garlic mixture, and the cumin. Taste for seasoning, and add salt, if needed. At this point, you can either serve the ful as is, or use an immersion blender to mash it to as chunky or smooth a consistency as you like.

Ladle the ful into serving bowls and top with parsley, red onion, radishes, tomatoes, and a drizzle of tahini. Serve warm, with pita bread on the side.

Chickpea-Flour Egg Bites
with Roasted Red Peppers

Just because you're vegan doesn't mean you have to be left out of the egg bite craze. These are made with a base of chickpea (or garbanzo bean) flour, which includes a good amount of protein (and fiber, too). Eat them straight from the Instant Pot for breakfast, or pack them for a mid-morning snack on the go.

———————

Grease a silicone egg bite mold generously with coconut oil. Pour 1 cup water into the Instant Pot.

In a blender, combine the almond milk, chickpea flour, egg replacer, nutritional yeast, coconut oil, salt, and turmeric. Blend at medium speed for about 1 minute, until smooth, then transfer to a bowl and let the batter rest for 10 minutes to thicken.

Stir in the bell pepper and parsley, then pour ¼ cup of the batter into each cup of the egg bite mold (they will be about three-quarters full). Place the filled mold on a wire metal steam rack, then cover the mold with a round of parchment paper to keep condensation from dripping onto the egg bites as they cook. Grasping the handles of the steam rack, lower the egg bites into the Instant Pot.

Secure the lid and set the Pressure Release to **Sealing**. Select the **Steam** setting and set the time for 10 minutes at high pressure. (The pot will take about 10 minutes to come up to pressure before the cooking program begins.)

When the cooking program ends, let the pressure release naturally for 10 minutes, then move the Pressure Release to **Venting** to release any remaining steam. Open the pot and, wearing heat-resistant mitts, grab the handles of the steam rack and lift the egg bite mold out of the pot. Let the bites cool in the mold for 5 minutes, then invert the mold onto a plate and lift off the mold. You may have to jiggle the mold a bit to release the bites.

Transfer the egg bites to plates and serve warm. You can also store them in an airtight container, refrigerated, for up to 3 days.

MAKES 7 BITES

1 cup almond milk

¾ cup chickpea flour

2 tablespoons egg replacer powder

1 tablespoon nutritional yeast

1 tablespoon coconut oil, plus more for greasing

¼ teaspoon fine sea salt

⅛ teaspoon ground turmeric

½ cup chopped roasted red bell pepper

1 tablespoon chopped fresh flat-leaf parsley

NOTES

Get creative with your egg bite fillings. Just keep the amount of mix-ins to about ½ cup. You can use any leftover roasted vegetables, shredded vegan cheese, sausage, and/or fresh herbs in place of the roasted bell peppers and parsley.

Various brands of silicone egg bite molds are available online. I purchased mine on Amazon. For a visual of the egg bite mold required for this recipe, see the green one shown in Essential Tools and Accessories (page 11).

CHAPTER 2

Grains and Pastas

Lemon Risotto with Pea Pistou

RISOTTO

¼ cup extra-virgin olive oil

2 shallots, minced

1½ cups Arborio rice

⅓ cup dry white wine

Juice of ½ large lemon

3 cups low-sodium vegetable broth (page 152)

¾ teaspoon fine sea salt

PISTOU

1 clove garlic

½ teaspoon fine sea salt

1 bunch chives
(about ¾ ounce)

½ cup frozen peas, thawed

Finely grated zest and juice of ½ large lemon

2 tablespoons extra-virgin olive oil

This risotto has springtime flair to spare, but you can make it any time of year—it uses frozen peas, rather than fresh ones. It's easy and fast to make (no stirring required), yet it has a sophisticated air. A big swirl of pistou is stirred in after cooking to keep the flavors bright, and it looks pretty, too.

To make the risotto: Select the **Sauté** setting on the Instant Pot, add the oil, and heat for 2 minutes. Add the shallots and sauté for about 4 minutes, until softened and just beginning to brown. Stir in the rice and sauté for 1 minute more. Stir in the wine and lemon juice and sauté for about 2 minutes, just until the liquid has evaporated and the rice begins to sizzle in the pot. Stir in the broth and salt. Scrape down the sides of the pot to make sure all of the rice is submerged in the broth.

Secure the lid and set the Pressure Release to **Sealing**. Press the **Cancel** button to reset the cooking program. Then select the **Manual** or **Pressure Cook** setting and set the cooking time for 5 minutes at high pressure. (The pot will take about 10 minutes to come up to pressure before the cooking program begins.)

While the risotto is cooking, make the pistou: Combine all of the pistou ingredients in a mini chopper or mortar and pestle. If using a mini chopper, process in 1-second pulses until the mixture becomes a fairly smooth puree. If using a mortar and pestle, first use the pestle to crush the garlic with the salt, then mash in the chives, then the peas, and finally stir in the lemon zest, lemon juice, and oil.

When the cooking program ends, let the pressure release naturally for 10 minutes, then move the Pressure Release to **Venting** to release any remaining steam. Open the pot and stir in the pistou, leaving some of it unincorporated so there are pockets of pistou throughout.

Spoon the risotto into bowls and serve immediately.

Winter Tabbouleh with Toasted Garlic and Kale

Traditional tabbouleh contains summer vegetables, but I like to make it in the wintertime, too. When tomatoes aren't at their best, I use lots of shredded lacinato (aka dino or dinosaur) kale instead. It's the dark green variety of kale that grows in bumpy, oblong leaves rather than wide, curly ones. Toasted garlic and warmly spicy cinnamon complement the kale in this hearty salad. Serve it on its own, as a side dish for a Mediterranean meal, or as the base of a grain bowl (page 158).

SERVES 4

3 tablespoons extra-virgin olive oil

2 cloves garlic, thinly sliced

1½ cups low-sodium vegetable broth (page 152)

1 cup coarse bulgur wheat

½ teaspoon ground cinnamon

½ teaspoon freshly ground black pepper

½ teaspoon fine sea salt, plus more as needed

1 large (8-ounce) bunch lacinato kale, stems removed, cut into ¼-inch-wide ribbons

2 tablespoons fresh lemon juice

Select the **Sauté** setting on the Instant Pot, add 1 tablespoon of the oil and the garlic, and heat for about 4 minutes, until the garlic has become toasty and brown but not burned. Add the broth, bulgur, cinnamon, pepper, and salt and stir to combine.

Secure the lid and set the Pressure Release to **Sealing**. Press the **Cancel** button to reset the cooking program. Then select the **Manual** or **Pressure Cook** setting and set the cooking time for 10 minutes at low pressure. (The pot will take about 5 minutes to come up to pressure before the cooking program begins.)

When the cooking program ends, let the pressure release naturally for 5 minutes, then move the Pressure Release to **Venting** to release the remaining steam. While the pressure is releasing, combine the kale and lemon juice in a large bowl. Use your hands to squeeze and massage the kale for about 2 minutes, until the leaves are wilted and darker in color.

Open the pot and use a fork to fluff the bulgur. Transfer the bulgur to the bowl with the kale and drizzle in the remaining 2 tablespoons of oil. Stir to combine. Taste for seasoning, adding more salt, if needed. Serve warm or chilled.

Buckwheat Pilaf with Mushrooms and Caramelized Onions

I think of buckwheat as the most savory of all grains. Get the whole-grain, roasted variety for this recipe—it's called kasha and it comes already roasted to bring out its deep nutty flavor. Mushrooms bump up the umami even further in this easy pilaf, and caramelized onions add depth and richness.

Select the **Sauté** setting on the Instant Pot, add the oil and garlic, and heat for 2 minutes, until the garlic is bubbling. Add the mushrooms and salt and sauté for 3 minutes, until the mushrooms are wilted. Stir in the broth, using a wooden spoon to nudge any browned bits from the bottom of the pot. Stir in the buckwheat, onions, and pepper, making sure all of the buckwheat is fully submerged in the broth.

Secure the lid and set the Pressure Release to **Sealing**. Press the **Cancel** button to reset the cooking program. Then select the **Manual** or **Pressure Cook** setting and set the cooking time for 15 minutes at high pressure. (The pot will take about 10 minutes to come up to pressure before the cooking program begins.)

When the cooking program ends, let the pressure release naturally for 10 minutes, then move the Pressure Release to **Venting** to release any remaining steam. Open the pot and use a fork to fluff the buckwheat. Spoon onto plates, garnish with parsley, and serve warm.

SERVES 6

2 tablespoons extra-virgin olive oil

2 cloves garlic, minced

8 ounces cremini and/or fresh shiitake mushroom caps, thinly sliced

½ teaspoon fine sea salt

1¾ cups low-sodium vegetable broth (page 152)

1½ cups whole roasted buckwheat groats (kasha)

½ cup caramelized onions (page 156)

½ teaspoon freshly ground black pepper

1 tablespoon chopped parsley

NOTES

If you can only find raw buckwheat groats, toast them in a dry skillet for a few minutes over medium heat to bring out their aroma.

If you have not already caramelized a batch of onions (page 156), start this recipe by sautéing 1 onion, thinly sliced, in the olive oil for 8 minutes before adding the garlic and mushrooms and continuing with the recipe. The onions will not be fully caramelized, but the pilaf will still come out delicious.

Speedy Penne Arrabbiata with Sheet Pan Meatballs

Vegetarian meatball recipes often involve separate cooking steps for the grains, beans, and vegetables, but I've combined all three in the Instant Pot to make these the easiest meatballs ever. Once the meatballs are in the oven, it's time to make your arrabbiata sauce and pasta all in the Instant Pot, too. Or skip the meatballs and just make the sauce for a simple pasta meal.

To make the meatballs: In a bowl, combine the red beans with 3 cups water and 1 teaspoon of the salt. Soak for 10 to 12 hours, then drain in a colander.

Select the **Sauté** setting on the Instant Pot, add the oil and garlic, and heat for 2 minutes, until the garlic is bubbling but not yet browned. Add the onion and sauté for 5 minutes, until the onion softens and the garlic turns golden brown. Add the mushrooms and sauté for 3 minutes more, until they are wilted and giving up their liquid. Add the tomato paste, soy sauce, and Italian seasoning, and sauté for 1 minute more.

Stir in the broth, beans, and rice, using a wooden spoon to nudge loose any browned bits from the bottom of the pot. Scrape down any grains of rice stuck to the sides of the pot, making sure the rice and beans are fully submerged in the broth.

Secure the lid and set the Pressure Release to **Sealing**. Press the **Cancel** button to reset the cooking program. Then select the **Manual, Pressure Cook,** or **Bean/Chili** setting and set the cooking time for 25 minutes at high pressure. (The pot will take about 5 minutes to come up to pressure before the cooking program begins.)

When the cooking program ends, let the pressure release naturally for 10 minutes, then move the Pressure Release to **Venting** to release any remaining steam. Open the pot and, wearing heat-resistant mitts, lift out the inner pot. Add the carrot, bread crumbs, walnuts, remaining ½ teaspoon salt, and pepper, and stir to combine. Let the mixture stand for 10 minutes to firm up and cool down a bit.

continued

SERVES 4 TO 6

MEATBALLS

¾ cup (4½ ounces) dried small red beans

1½ teaspoons fine sea salt

3 tablespoons extra-virgin olive oil

3 cloves garlic, minced

1 small yellow onion, finely chopped

4 ounces (about 6 medium) cremini or button mushrooms, finely chopped

1 tablespoon tomato paste

1 tablespoon soy sauce, tamari, or coconut aminos

1 teaspoon Italian seasoning

2 cups low-sodium vegetable broth (page 152)

¾ cup medium- or long-grain brown rice

1 large carrot, finely shredded (use a coarse Microplane)

¾ cup panko bread crumbs

½ cup walnut halves and pieces, toasted and chopped

¼ teaspoon freshly ground black pepper

Speedy Penne Arrabbiata with Sheet Pan Meatballs, continued

Speedy Penne Arrabbiata with Sheet Pan Meatballs, continued

ARRABBIATA SAUCE

¼ cup extra-virgin olive oil

2 cloves garlic, minced

1 (28-ounce) can whole San Marzano tomatoes

4 pickled hot chile peppers or pepperoncini, minced

2 teaspoons Italian seasoning

1 teaspoon fine sea salt

½ teaspoon red pepper flakes

1 pound penne pasta

3½ cups water

¼ cup chopped fresh flat-leaf parsley

NOTES

You can make the meatballs ahead of time, if you like. Let them cool to room temperature after baking, then store in the freezer for up to 2 months. When you're ready to serve, microwave them a few at a time on a plate in a single layer for 2 to 3 minutes.

The meatball recipe also works great for veggie burgers. Just use a ½-cup measure to scoop eight portions onto the baking sheet, then flatten and bake for 20 minutes.

While the meatball mixture is cooling, preheat the oven to 375°F. Line a baking sheet with parchment paper or a silicone mat and grease it lightly with olive oil or nonstick cooking spray.

Use a small (1½-tablespoon) cookie scoop to portion the meatball mixture out onto the baking sheet. Bake the meatballs for 20 minutes, until they are lightly browned and crispy on the outside.

To make the sauce: While the meatballs are baking, press the **Cancel** button to reset the cooking program. Then select the **Sauté** setting, add the oil and garlic, and heat for about 3 minutes, until the garlic turns golden but is not browned. Add the tomatoes and their liquid, crushing the tomatoes with your hands as you add them to the pot. Stir in the chile peppers, Italian seasoning, salt, and red pepper flakes. Let the sauce cook for 10 minutes more, stirring occasionally. At this point, you can use the sauce as is, store it in the fridge for up to 1 week, freeze for up to 6 months, or add pasta and water for a one-pot dish.

To make a one-pot dish: Add the pasta and water to the sauce and stir well. Secure the lid and set the Pressure Release to **Sealing**. Press the **Cancel** button to reset the cooking program. Then select the **Manual** or **Pressure Cook** setting and set the cooking time for 5 minutes at high pressure. (The pot will take about 15 minutes to come up to pressure before the cooking program begins.)

When the cooking program ends, let the pressure release naturally for 5 minutes, then move the Pressure Release to **Venting** to release any remaining steam. Open the pot and give the pasta and sauce a good stir. Spoon the pasta into bowls, top with the meatballs, sprinkle with parsley, and serve.

Mexican-Style Rice or Quinoa

It really only takes a few extra minutes and a handful of spices to transform basic grains into a Mexican-style treat. It's great folded into burritos, as the base for grain bowls, and as a side dish with tacos or any other Mexican or Tex-Mex meal.

———————

Select the **Sauté** setting on the Instant Pot, add the oil and garlic, and heat for about 2 minutes, until the garlic is bubbling. Stir in the rice or quinoa, chili powder, coriander, cumin, salt, and broth, using a wooden spoon to nudge any browned bits from the bottom of the pot. Scrape down any grains that are stuck to the sides of the pot, making sure the grains are fully submerged in the broth. Add the tomato paste in a dollop on top of the grains. Do not stir.

Secure the lid and set the Pressure Release to **Sealing**. Press the **Cancel** button to reset the cooking program. Then select the **Manual** or **Pressure Cook** setting and set the cooking time for 15 minutes at low pressure for rice, or 12 minutes at low pressure for quinoa. (The pot will take about 5 minutes to come up to pressure before the cooking program begins.)

When the cooking program ends, let the pressure release naturally for 10 minutes, then move the Pressure Release to **Venting** to release any remaining steam. Open the pot and, wearing heat-resistant mitts, lift out the inner pot. Add the lime juice, then use a fork to fluff the grains and serve.

SERVES 6

2 tablespoons extra-virgin olive oil

2 cloves garlic, minced

1½ cups long-grain white rice or quinoa, rinsed and drained

1 tablespoon chili powder

1 teaspoon ground coriander

1 teaspoon ground cumin

1 teaspoon fine sea salt

1½ cups low-sodium vegetable broth (page 152)

2 tablespoons tomato paste

1 tablespoon fresh lime juice

Mac 'n' Trees

I'm so thankful to live in a time when we're using cashews as the base for so many creamy vegan sauces. The sauce for this macaroni is creamy and a little tangy, just like the boxed versions of my childhood. If you like, you can soak the nuts overnight in the refrigerator; then the sauce will come together in a couple of minutes while the pasta is cooking in the Instant Pot.

———————

To make the macaroni: Add the pasta, water, and salt to the Instant Pot. Use a spoon or spatula to spread the pasta in an even layer, making sure it is all submerged in the water.

Secure the lid and set the Pressure Release to **Sealing**. Select the **Manual** or **Pressure Cook** setting and set the cooking time for 6 minutes at high pressure. (The pot will take about 15 minutes to come up to pressure before the cooking program begins.)

To make the sauce: While the pasta is cooking, combine the cashews, water, nutritional yeast, lemon juice, garlic, mustard, Tabasco, salt, and cayenne in a blender. Blend at high speed for about 1 minute, until smooth, scraping down the sides of the blender halfway through, if necessary. Taste for seasoning, adding more salt and/or cayenne, if needed. You can also add an extra splash of water, if you prefer a thinner sauce.

When the cooking program ends, let the pressure release naturally for 5 minutes, then move the Pressure Release to **Venting** to release any remaining steam. Open the pot and stir in the sauce.

Spoon the macaroni into bowls and serve immediately.

SERVES 4 TO 6

MACARONI

1 pound elbow macaroni

4 cups water

1 teaspoon fine sea salt

SAUCE

1 cup raw cashews, soaked in water for 2 hours at room temperature, or up to overnight in the refrigerator, and drained

⅓ cup water, plus more if needed

2 tablespoons nutritional yeast

1½ tablespoons fresh lemon juice

1 clove garlic, peeled

1 teaspoon prepared yellow mustard

1 teaspoon Tabasco sauce

½ teaspoon fine sea salt, plus more as needed

¼ teaspoon cayenne pepper, plus more as needed

NOTE

To make a crispy bread crumb topping, as shown, toss together 1 cup panko bread crumbs with 1 tablespoon olive oil. Toast the bread crumbs in a skillet over medium heat for a few minutes, until golden brown.

Polenta with Black Pepper

SERVES 4

4 cups low-sodium vegetable broth (page 152)

3 tablespoons extra-virgin olive oil, plus more for serving

1 cup coarse polenta (not an instant or quick-cooking variety)

¾ teaspoon freshly ground black pepper, plus more for serving

¼ teaspoon fine sea salt, plus more as needed

NOTES

Add extra flavor to your polenta by sautéing garlic, onions, or mushrooms in the oil before adding the broth. Fresh or dried herbs are great, too. Try sage, rosemary, or thyme.

Wash the Instant Pot lid and inner pot immediately after use. They're much easier to clean before the polenta has had a chance to dry out.

If you've ever made polenta, you know it requires a lot of stirring and attention. Not so with the Instant Pot. This low-maintenance version is flavored simply with olive oil, salt, and pepper, so it makes a versatile side dish. It can also be its own course, served with a ladleful of store-bought or homemade marinara or arrabbiata sauce (page 42).

Select the **Sauté** setting on the Instant Pot. Add the broth and oil, then cover the pot with the glass lid and cook just until it begins to simmer, 8 to 10 minutes. Whisking constantly, pour the polenta into the broth in a thin stream. Press the **Cancel** button to reset the cooking program.

Secure the lid and set the Pressure Release to **Sealing**. Select the **Manual, Pressure Cook,** or **Porridge** setting and set the cooking time for 10 minutes at high pressure. (The pot will take about 5 minutes to come up to pressure before the cooking program begins.)

When the cooking program ends, let the pressure release naturally for 15 minutes, then move the Pressure Release to **Venting** to release any remaining steam. Open the pot and, wearing heat-resistant mitts, lift out the inner pot. The polenta will have some liquid on the top; stir to incorporate the liquid, using a wooden spoon to scrape along the bottom of the pot to loosen any stuck polenta. If there are any lumps, break them up with a whisk. Stir in the pepper and salt. Taste for seasoning and add more salt, if needed.

Spoon the polenta into bowls, drizzle with oil, and top with a few grinds of pepper. Serve piping hot.

Jalapeño Cornbread

SERVES 8

2 tablespoons egg replacer powder

1 cup plus 2 tablespoons unsweetened nondairy milk

1½ cups finely ground cornmeal

⅔ cup all-purpose flour

2 teaspoons baking powder

1 teaspoon fine sea salt

¼ cup vegan shortening, melted (I recommend Nutiva or Earth Balance brand)

1 jalapeño chile, seeded and diced

A no-brainer accompaniment for Summer Vegetable Chili (page 85), this cornbread can be made without heating up your kitchen. Studded with fresh diced jalapeño, it's moist and flavorful with a little spicy kick. Cut it into wedges and serve it right away—it's best when it's still steaming hot, straight out of the pot.

———————

Grease the sides of a 7-inch springform or cake pan and line the base of the pan with a round of parchment paper. Pour 1 cup water into the Instant Pot.

In a small bowl, stir together the egg replacer and nondairy milk. Set aside for a minute to thicken.

In a mixing bowl, whisk together the cornmeal, flour, baking powder, and salt. Add the egg replacer mixture and shortening and stir just until the dry ingredients are fully incorporated. Fold in the jalapeño. The batter will be very thick.

Transfer the batter to the lined pan and spread it out in an even layer, then cover the pan tightly with aluminum foil. Place the pan on a long-handled silicone steam rack. Holding the handles of the steam rack, lift the pan and lower it into the pot.

Secure the lid and set the Pressure Release to **Sealing**. Select the **Manual, Pressure Cook,** or **Cake** setting and set the cooking time for 35 minutes at high pressure. (The pot will take about 10 minutes to come up to pressure before the cooking program begins.)

When the cooking program ends, let the pressure release naturally for 10 minutes, then move the Pressure Release to **Venting** to release any remaining steam. Open the pot and, wearing heat-resistant mitts, grab the handles of the steam rack, lift the pan out of the pot, and set the pan on a cooling rack. Remove the aluminum foil, taking care not to let any condensation that has settled on top of the foil drop onto the bread.

Let the cornbread rest in the pan for 5 minutes, then run a knife around the edge of the bread to loosen it from the pan sides. Invert the pan on top of the cooling rack to unmold the bread, peel off the parchment, place a plate on top of the bread, then flip it back over so it is right side up on the serving plate. Cut the bread into wedges and serve steaming hot.

NOTE

For a gluten-free variation, substitute Bob's Red Mill Paleo Flour or another gluten-free flour blend for the all-purpose flour.

CHAPTER 3

Beans and Lentils

Greek-Style Lima Beans
with Almond Feta

In Greece, a dish similar to this one is made with *gigantes* beans. I love to use lima beans instead, since they're easy to find at most grocery stores, and they usually cost much less than other large white beans. Even better, they cook in less time, even with tomatoes in the mix. You can serve the beans on their own, but they're even better topped with almond feta.

1½ teaspoons fine sea salt

1¼ cups (8 ounces) dried large lima beans

3 tablespoons extra-virgin olive oil, plus more for serving

2 cloves garlic, minced

1 yellow onion, diced

2 celery stalks, diced

1 teaspoon dried oregano

¼ teaspoon freshly ground black pepper, plus more for serving

2 cups low-sodium vegetable broth (page 152)

1 (14½-ounce) can diced tomatoes

¾ cup Almond Feta (page 115)

2 tablespoons chopped fresh flat-leaf parsley

Crusty bread for serving

In a bowl, stir together 4 cups water and 1 teaspoon of the salt. Add the beans and let soak for at least 8 hours, or up to overnight. Drain the beans and set aside.

Select the **Sauté** setting on the Instant Pot, add the oil and garlic, and heat for 2 minutes, until the garlic is bubbling. Add the onion, celery, oregano, pepper, and the remaining ½ teaspoon salt. Sauté for 5 minutes, until the onions soften and become translucent. Stir in the beans and the broth, using a wooden spoon to nudge loose any browned bits from the bottom of the pot. Pour in the tomatoes and their liquid, leaving them on top of the other ingredients. Do not stir.

Secure the lid and set the Pressure Release to **Sealing**. Press the **Cancel** button to reset the cooking program. Then select the **Manual, Pressure Cook,** or **Bean/Chili** setting and set the cooking time for 40 minutes at high pressure. (The pot will take about 15 minutes to come up to pressure before the cooking program begins.)

When the cooking program ends, let the pressure release naturally for at least 35 minutes, then move the Pressure Release to **Venting** to release any remaining steam. Open the pot and stir the beans.

Ladle the beans into serving bowls. Spoon or sprinkle the feta on top of the beans, then drizzle with oil. Add a few grinds of pepper and the parsley. Serve hot, with crusty bread alongside.

BBQ "Baked" Beans

SERVES 8

1 tablespoon fine sea salt

2½ cups (1 pound) dried great Northern beans

1¾ cups water

1 cup barbecue sauce (I recommend Annie's Naturals brand)

¼ cup prepared yellow mustard

2 tablespoons maple syrup

1½ teaspoons freshly ground black pepper

1½ teaspoons smoked paprika

3 tablespoons avocado oil or other neutral oil

1 large yellow onion, diced

2 cloves garlic, minced

1 bay leaf

The next time you're invited to a potluck or cookout, offer to bring the baked beans. These are sweet and smoky, and the list of ingredients isn't a mile long. I rely on store-bought barbecue sauce to kick-start the flavor, then jazz it up with a few pantry staples.

In a large bowl, stir together 6 cups water and the salt. Add the beans and let soak for at least 8 hours, or up to overnight. Drain the beans and set aside.

In a liquid measuring cup or small bowl, stir together the water, barbecue sauce, mustard, maple syrup, pepper, and smoked paprika.

Select the **Sauté** setting on the Instant Pot, add the oil, and heat for 2 minutes. Add the onion and sauté for about 10 minutes, stirring often, until it begins to caramelize. Add the garlic and sauté for about 2 minutes more, until the garlic is no longer raw. Add the barbecue sauce mixture, beans, and bay leaf. Stir to combine, using a wooden spoon to nudge loose any browned bits from the bottom of the pot.

Secure the lid and set the Pressure Release to **Sealing**. Press the **Cancel** button to reset the cooking program. Then select the **Manual, Pressure Cook,** or **Bean/Chili** setting and set the cooking time for 40 minutes at high pressure. (The pot will take about 20 minutes to come up to pressure before the cooking program begins.)

When the cooking program ends, let the pressure release naturally for 35 minutes, then move the Pressure Release to **Venting** to release any remaining steam. Open the pot, stir the beans, and discard the bay leaf.

Ladle the beans into bowls and serve hot. The beans will keep in an airtight container, refrigerated, for up to 3 days.

Roasted Garlic Hummus

The sweet, mellow flavor of roasted garlic makes for a delicious hummus. You can cook your chickpeas straight from dried, then blitz them in the food processor while they're warm for an extra-smooth dip. Serve the hummus with crudités, in pita pockets, or spread generously on a slice of whole-grain bread.

————————

Add the water, chickpeas, and 1 teaspoon of the salt to the Instant Pot. Secure the lid and set the Pressure Release to **Sealing**. Select the **Manual, Pressure Cook,** or **Bean/Chili** setting and set the cooking time for 40 minutes at high pressure. (The pot will take about 15 minutes to come up to pressure before the cooking program begins.)

When the cooking program ends, let the pressure release naturally for 15 minutes, then move the Pressure Release to **Venting** to release any remaining steam. Open the pot and ladle out and reserve ¾ cup of the cooking liquid. Wearing heat-resistant mitts, lift out the inner pot and drain the chickpeas in a colander.

Transfer the warm drained chickpeas to a food processor or blender. Add the reserved cooking liquid, the roasted garlic, tahini, lemon juice, cumin, smoked paprika, and remaining 1 teaspoon salt. Process at medium speed for about 1 minute, until the mixture is smooth and creamy.

Spoon the hummus into the center of a wide, shallow serving bowl and spread it out into a thick circle. Sprinkle with the sweet paprika and drizzle with the olive oil and serve. The hummus will keep in an airtight container, refrigerated, for up to 3 days.

MAKES ABOUT
3½ CUPS

4 cups water

1 cup (8 ounces) dried chickpeas

2 teaspoons fine sea salt

1 bulb roasted garlic cloves (page 156)

½ cup tahini

3 tablespoons fresh lemon juice

¼ teaspoon ground cumin

¼ teaspoon smoked paprika

¼ teaspoon sweet paprika

1 tablespoon extra-virgin olive oil

NOTES

If you prefer to soak before cooking, soak your chickpeas overnight and reduce the cooking time to 25 minutes at high pressure, with a 15-minute timed pressure release.

For a more traditional hummus, substitute 2 cloves of raw garlic, chopped, for the head of roasted garlic.

White Bean and Carrot Tagine

SERVES 8

2½ cups (1 pound) dried great Northern beans

¼ cup extra-virgin olive oil, plus more for serving

4 cloves garlic, minced

1 yellow onion, sliced

3 cups low-sodium vegetable broth (page 152)

1 pound (8 medium) carrots, peeled and cut into ½-inch rounds

1½ tablespoons ras el hanout (see Note)

1 tablespoon tomato paste

1 tablespoon fresh lemon juice

2 tablespoons chopped fresh mint

Couscous or flatbread for serving

NOTE

If you don't have ras el hanout, make your own by combining 2 teaspoons paprika, ½ teaspoon ground cinnamon, ½ teaspoon ground coriander, ½ teaspoon ground cumin, and ¼ teaspoon cayenne pepper.

Ras el hanout is one of my favorite spice blends, and it works well in this Moroccan-inspired stew of great Northern beans and soft, silky carrots. Recipes vary for the spice blend (my favorite comes from Oaktown Spice Shop), but it's always warmly sweet with paprika, cinnamon, and at least a hint of heat. Serve the tagine over couscous or with flatbread on the side.

_____

In a bowl, combine the beans with 4 cups water and 1 teaspoon of the salt. Let soak for 10 to 12 hours, or overnight. Drain the beans and set aside.

Select the **Sauté** setting on the Instant Pot, add the oil and garlic, and heat for 2 minutes, until the garlic is bubbling but not browned. Add the onion and sauté for 5 minutes, until the onion is softened and the garlic is toasty and brown. Stir in the broth and use a wooden spoon to nudge loose any browned bits from the bottom of the pot. Stir in the carrots, ras el hanout, and the remaining 1 teaspoon salt. Stir in the beans, making sure all of the beans are submerged in the cooking liquid.

Secure the lid and set the Pressure Release to **Sealing**. Press the **Cancel** button to reset the cooking program. Then select the **Manual, Pressure Cook,** or **Bean/Chili** setting and set the cooking time for 30 minutes at high pressure. (The pot will take about 15 minutes to come up to pressure before the cooking program begins.)

When the cooking program ends, let the pressure release naturally (this will take about 40 minutes). Open the pot and stir in the tomato paste and lemon juice. Taste and adjust the seasoning with salt, if needed.

Ladle the tagine into bowls. Drizzle with oil and sprinkle with mint. Serve hot, with couscous or flatbread.

Braised Beluga Lentils with Kale and Carrots

SERVES 6

¼ cup extra-virgin olive oil, plus more for serving

2 shallots, diced

5 cloves garlic, minced

½ teaspoon red pepper flakes

½ teaspoon ground nutmeg

1 teaspoon fine sea salt, plus more as needed

2 bunches (about 1 pound) lacinato or curly kale, stems discarded and leaves chopped into 1-inch pieces, or one 1 (10-ounce) bag washed and trimmed baby kale, cut into 1-inch pieces

2 large carrots, peeled and diced

2½ cups water

1 cup beluga lentils, rinsed

Crusty bread for serving

The ingredient list for this recipe is simple, yet you end up with a lentil dish that tastes luxurious and complex. Beluga lentils are black and resemble caviar. Kale and carrots both take on a silky texture, and a generous amount of olive oil really makes it—resist the urge to use less, even if it sounds like a lot. This is an adaptation of the version served at Buvette in New York City, minus the hours of simmering on the stove top.

Select the **Sauté** setting on the Instant Pot, add the oil, and heat for 1 minute. Add the shallots and garlic and sauté for about 4 minutes, until the shallots soften. Add the red pepper flakes, nutmeg, and salt and sauté for 1 minute more. Stir in the kale and carrots and sauté for about 3 minutes, until the kale fully wilts. Stir in the water and lentils, scraping down the sides of the pot to make sure the lentils are submerged.

Secure the lid and set the Pressure Release to **Sealing**. Press the **Cancel** button to reset the cooking program. Then select the **Manual, Pressure Cook,** or **Bean/Chili** setting and set the cooking time for 30 minutes at high pressure. (The pot will take about 10 minutes to come up to pressure before the cooking program begins.)

When the cooking program ends, let the pressure release naturally for 10 minutes, then move the Pressure Release to **Venting** to release any remaining steam. Open the pot and give the mixture a stir. Taste and adjust the seasoning with salt, if needed.

Ladle the lentils into serving dishes and drizzle with oil. Serve warm, with crusty bread alongside.

Green Lentil Sloppy Joes

These take me right back to summer camp, when the camp counselors made us an easy dinner of Sloppy Joes on kaiser rolls. I'm 100 percent sure they used industrial-sized cans of Manwich, but these days I'm all for packing in lots of vegetables and making a big pot of nourishing lentils instead. Add some whole-wheat buns, sweet onion slices, and pickles and you've got a deliciously retro dinner, reinvented for the twenty-first century.

———————————

Select the **Sauté** setting on the Instant Pot, add the oil, and heat for 2 minutes. Add the onion, bell pepper, carrot, celery, and garlic and sauté for about 10 minutes, until the onion is translucent but not yet beginning to brown. Add the chili powder, salt, pepper, cumin, and smoked paprika, and sauté for 1 minute. Add the Worcestershire, vinegar, broth, and lentils and stir well. Add the sugar, tomato sauce, and tomato paste on top of the other ingredients. Do not stir.

Secure the lid and set the Pressure Release to **Sealing**. Press the **Cancel** button to reset the cooking program. Then select the **Manual, Pressure Cook,** or **Bean/Chili** setting and set the cooking time for 25 minutes at high pressure. (The pot will take about 10 minutes to come up to pressure before the cooking program begins.)

When the cooking program ends, let the pressure release naturally for at least 10 minutes, then move the Pressure Release to **Venting** to release any remaining steam. Open the pot and stir to incorporate the tomato paste.

Place the bun bottoms, cut side up, on individual plates and ladle the Sloppy Joe mixture onto the buns. Top with the onions and pickles, close with the bun tops, and serve hot.

SERVES 8

¼ cup extra-virgin olive oil

1 yellow onion, diced

1 green bell pepper, seeded and diced

1 large carrot, peeled and diced

2 stalks celery, diced

3 cloves garlic minced

1 tablespoon chili powder

1 teaspoon fine sea salt

½ teaspoon freshly ground black pepper

½ teaspoon ground cumin

½ teaspoon smoked paprika

2 tablespoons vegan Worcestershire sauce

1 tablespoon cider vinegar

4 cups low-sodium vegetable broth (page 152)

2¼ cups (1 pound) green lentils, rinsed

¼ cup turbinado or organic cane sugar

1 (15-ounce) can tomato sauce

¼ cup tomato paste

8 whole-wheat hamburger buns, split and toasted

8 sweet yellow onion slices

Bread-and-butter pickle slices for serving

Puy Lentil Salad with French Vinaigrette

Protein-packed lentils can be enjoyed in cold dishes as well as hot ones, and the Puy variety in particular holds its shape well when cooked under pressure. This makes it a great base for salads. This recipe is French-inspired, with a Dijon mustard and herb vinaigrette and lots of crunchy vegetables. Served warm or cool, as a side dish or over greens, it's one of my favorite ways to enjoy these quick-cooking legumes.

———————————

To make the lentils: In a 1½-quart stainless-steel bowl, stir together the lentils, 1½ cups of the water, and the salt. Pour the remaining 2 cups water into the Instant Pot and place a tall steam rack in the pot. Put the bowl on the steam rack. Select the **Manual** or **Pressure Cook** setting and set the cooking time for 20 minutes at high pressure.

While the lentils are cooking, make the vinaigrette: In a jar with a tight-fitting lid or other leakproof container, combine the oil, lemon juice, sugar, shallot, mustard, herbes de Provence, salt, and pepper. Cover and shake vigorously. Set aside.

When the cooking program ends, perform a quick pressure release by moving the Pressure Release to **Venting**. Open the pot and, wearing heat-resistant mitts, remove the bowl of lentils. Drain the lentils in a colander, then return them to the bowl. While they are still warm, pour half of the vinaigrette over the lentils and stir gently. Let cool for 20 minutes.

In a serving bowl, toss together the lentils, carrot, celery, bell pepper, onion, and parsley. Taste and add more vinaigrette and/or salt as needed. Serve the salad at room temperature, or cover and chill for up to 2 days before serving.

SERVES 4 TO 6

LENTILS

1 cup French green (Puy) lentils, rinsed

3½ cups water

½ teaspoon fine sea salt

VINAIGRETTE

½ cup extra-virgin olive oil

¼ cup fresh lemon juice

1½ teaspoons turbinado or organic cane sugar

1 small shallot, minced

2 teaspoons Dijon mustard

1 teaspoon dried herbes de Provence

½ teaspoon fine sea salt, plus more as needed

½ teaspoon freshly ground black pepper

1 large carrot, diced

2 ribs celery, diced

1 red bell pepper, diced

½ small red onion, diced

¼ cup chopped fresh flat-leaf parsley

NOTE

Beluga lentils are a good substitute for Puy lentils.

Chana Masala

SERVES 4

1⅛ cup (8 ounces) dried chickpeas

4¼ cups water

1 teaspoon fine sea salt

2 cups Indian Simmer Sauce (recipe follows)

1 tablespoon fresh lemon juice

Hot steamed rice (page 146) or warmed naan for serving

Indian simmer sauces are available in most grocery stores, but it can be hard to track down a vegan variety (Maya Kaimal brand Goan Coconut Indian Simmer Sauce is a good one). The recipe that follows will yield sauce to spare, enough for three batches of this spicy chana masala, so you can freeze the extra for a later date. If you're pressed for time, use two drained cans of chickpeas (garbanzo beans) instead of dried ones, or, when cooking the dried chickpeas, follow the quick-soaking method used for the Chickpea Salad Sandwiches with Aquafaba Mayonnaise (page 100).

———————

Combine the chickpeas, 4 cups of the water, and salt in the Instant Pot. Select the **Manual, Pressure Cook,** or **Bean/Chili** setting and set the cooking time for 15 minutes at high pressure; select the **Timer** or **Delay** function and set the time delay for 10 hours. (When the soaking time is complete, the pot will take about 15 minutes to come up to pressure before the cooking program begins.)

When the cooking program ends, let the pressure release naturally for at least 15 minutes, then move the Pressure Release to **Venting** to release any remaining steam. Open the pot and, wearing heat-resistant mitts, lift the inner pot out of the housing and drain the chickpeas, reserving the cooking liquid if you wish to make recipes with aquafaba; see page 100. Return the cooked chickpeas to the inner pot and return to the Instant Pot housing. Press the **Cancel** button to reset the cooking program.

Add the simmer sauce and the remaining ¼ cup water to the pot and stir well. Secure the lid and set the Pressure Release to **Sealing**. Select the **Manual** or **Pressure Cook** setting and set the cooking time for 3 minutes at high pressure. (The pot will take about 10 minutes to come up to pressure before the cooking program begins.)

When the cooking program ends, let the pressure release naturally for at least 15 minutes, then move the Pressure Release to **Venting** to release any remaining steam. Open the pot, add the lemon juice, and give the mixture a final stir.

Ladle the chana masala into bowls and serve hot, with rice or naan.

INDIAN SIMMER SAUCE
MAKES ABOUT 6 CUPS

2 tablespoons avocado oil or other neutral oil

3 large yellow onions, finely diced

2 cloves garlic, minced

1-inch knob fresh ginger, peeled and grated

1 teaspoon fine sea salt

4 teaspoons ground coriander

1 tablespoon ground cumin

1 tablespoon garam masala

1 tablespoon paprika

½ teaspoon cayenne pepper

½ teaspoon ground turmeric

1 cup water

1 (28-ounce) can whole tomatoes

Select the **Sauté** setting on the Instant Pot, add the oil, and heat for 2 minutes. Add the onions, garlic, ginger, and salt and sauté until the onions soften, give up their liquid, and are just beginning to brown and stick to the pot, about 15 minutes. Stir in the coriander, cumin, garam masala, paprika, cayenne, and turmeric and sauté for 1 minute more. Stir in the water, using a wooden spoon to nudge loose any browned bits from the bottom of the pot. Add the tomatoes and their liquid, leaving the tomatoes whole.

Secure the lid and set the Pressure Release to **Sealing**. Press the **Cancel** button to reset the cooking program. Then select the **Manual** or **Pressure Cook** setting and set the cooking time for 15 minutes at high pressure. (The pot will take about 10 minutes to come up to pressure before the cooking program begins.)

When the cooking program ends, let the pressure release naturally (this will take about 25 minutes). Open the pot and, using the wooden spoon, smash the tomatoes against the side of the pot to break them up into the sauce. Wearing heat-resistant mitts, remove the inner pot from the housing and let the sauce cool.

Set aside 2 cups of sauce for the chana masala and transfer the rest of the sauce to an airtight container and refrigerate for up to 3 days. To freeze the sauce, transfer 2-cup portions to quart-size ziplock plastic freezer bags and freeze for up to 4 months.

Yellow Mung Bean (Moong Dal) and Spinach Curry

SERVES 4

3½ cups water

1 cup yellow lentils (moong dal), rinsed

1½ teaspoons fine sea salt, plus more as needed

3 tablespoons coconut oil

1 teaspoon cumin seeds

1 yellow onion, thinly sliced

1 jalapeño chile, seeded and diced

3 cloves garlic, thinly sliced

1 Roma tomato, diced

1 teaspoon ground coriander

½ teaspoon ground turmeric

¼ teaspoon cayenne pepper

¼ cup chopped fresh cilantro

1 (5- to 6-ounce) bag baby spinach

Hot steamed rice (page 146) or warmed naan for serving

NOTE

If you prefer your dal with a thinner consistency, stir in hot water after cooking, along with the spices, cilantro, and spinach.

Dal and rice is one of my favorite meals, an Indian comfort food that's quick-cooking, filling, and easy to make. You can find yellow lentils (moong dal) in Indian grocery stores and online. While the lentils cook in the Instant Pot, aromatic spices and vegetables simmer together in a skillet on the stove. Baby spinach is stirred in at the end of cooking, so you get your greens and protein all in one dish.

———————————

Add the water, mung beans, and salt to the Instant Pot. Secure the lid and set the Pressure Release to **Sealing**. Select the **Manual, Pressure Cook,** or **Bean/Chili** setting and set the cooking time for 5 minutes at high pressure. (The pot will take about 10 minutes to come up to pressure before the cooking program begins.)

While the mung beans are cooking, in a large skillet over medium-high heat, melt the coconut oil. Add the cumin seeds and cook, stirring, until toasty and fragrant, about 1 minute. Add the onion and jalapeño and sauté for about 4 minutes, until the onion softens. Nudge the mixture to the sides of the skillet. Add the garlic to the center of the skillet and sauté for about 2 minutes, until the garlic is browned but not burnt. Add the tomato and sauté for about 3 minutes, mixing in the ingredients from the sides of the skillet and scraping up any browned bits from the bottom of the skillet. Remove the skillet from the heat and stir in the coriander, turmeric, and cayenne. Set aside.

When the cooking program ends, let the pressure release naturally for 10 minutes, then move the Pressure Release to **Venting** to release any remaining steam. Open the pot and add the mixture from the skillet along with the cilantro and the spinach, then stir to combine. Taste and adjust the seasoning with salt, if needed.

Ladle the curry into bowls and serve piping hot, with rice or naan.

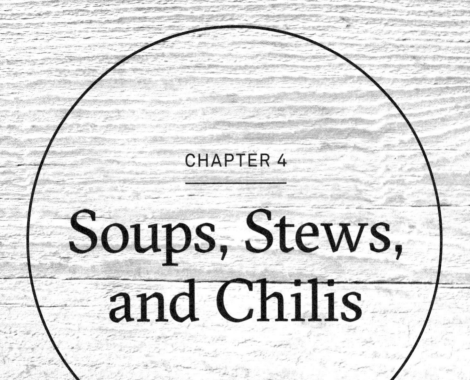

CHAPTER 4

Soups, Stews, and Chilis

Artichoke Soup with Garlic Bread Croutons

SERVES 4 AS A
FIRST COURSE

SOUP

2 tablespoons extra-virgin olive oil

2 cloves garlic, minced

1 large shallot, thinly sliced

2 ribs celery, thinly sliced

½ teaspoon fine sea salt, plus more as needed

¼ teaspoon freshly ground black pepper

1 cup low-sodium vegetable broth (page 152)

1 (12-ounce) bag frozen artichoke hearts

1 cup unsweetened nondairy milk

GARLIC BREAD CROUTONS

½ sourdough baguette, cut into ¾-inch slices

1 clove garlic, cut in half

1 tablespoon extra-virgin olive oil

Lemon wedges for serving

This creamy, silky soup is just like the version at Duarte's Tavern in Pescadero, California (minus the dairy, of course). If you haven't tried artichoke soup before, you've definitely got to give this Central Coast specialty a try. Serve it with garlic bread croutons for dipping and swiping up the last drops of soup.

———————————

To make the soup: Select the **Sauté** setting on the Instant Pot, add the oil and garlic, and heat for 2 minutes, until the garlic is bubbling but not browned. Add the shallot, celery, salt, and pepper and sauté for 3 minutes, until the shallots are softened.

Stir in the broth, using a wooden spoon to nudge any browned bits from the bottom of the pot. Add the artichokes in an even layer. They do not need to be completely submerged in the broth.

Secure the lid and set the Pressure Release to **Sealing**. Press the **Cancel** button to reset the cooking program. Then select the **Manual** or **Pressure Cook** setting and set the cooking time for 5 minutes at high pressure. (The pot will take about 10 minutes to come up to pressure before the cooking program begins.)

While the soup is cooking, make the garlic bread croutons: Rub the baguette slices with the cut sides of the garlic clove, then drizzle the bread with the oil. Toast in a toaster oven or under a broiler until golden brown, about 5 minutes. Set aside.

When the cooking program ends, perform a quick pressure release by moving the Pressure Release to **Venting**. Open the pot and, wearing heat-resistant mitts, remove the inner pot from the housing and pour the contents into a blender. Add the nondairy milk and puree until smooth. Taste for seasoning and add more salt, if needed.

Pour the soup into bowls and serve warm, with the croutons and lemon wedges on the side.

Minestrone con Riso

A good minestrone should be chock-full of vegetables, with a light, tomatoey broth and some sort of starch to add heartiness. In this pressure cooker version, I prefer to include rice, since it holds up better than pasta (see Note if you want to use potatoes instead). Serve the soup with some olive oil–drizzled bread for a more filling meal.

———————————

Select the **Sauté** setting on the Instant Pot, add the oil, and heat for 1 minute. Add the onion, carrot, celery, salt, and pepper and sauté for about 5 minutes, until the onion softens but is not browned. Add the cabbage, zucchini, beans, tomatoes and their liquid, broth, rice, Italian seasoning, and bay leaf and stir well. It's fine if the vegetables aren't fully submerged, as they will release their own liquid as they cook.

Secure the lid and set the Pressure Release to **Sealing**. Press the **Cancel** button to reset the cooking program. Then select the **Manual** or **Pressure Cook** setting and set the cooking time for 5 minutes at high pressure. (The pot will take about 20 minutes to come up to pressure before the cooking program begins.)

When the cooking program ends, let the pressure release naturally for 15 minutes, then move the Pressure Release to **Venting** to release any remaining steam. Open the pot, remove and discard the bay leaf, and stir in the parsley.

Ladle the soup into bowls and serve piping hot.

SERVES 6 TO 8

2 tablespoons extra-virgin olive oil

1 yellow onion, diced

1 carrot, diced

2 celery stalks, diced

½ teaspoon fine sea salt

¼ teaspoon freshly ground black pepper

¼ head green cabbage, cored and chopped

2 zucchini, diced

1½ cups cooked cannellini or kidney beans (page 144), or 1 (15-ounce) can cannellini or kidney beans, rinsed and drained

1 (14½-ounce) can diced tomatoes

4 cups low-sodium vegetable broth (page 152)

½ cup long-grain white rice

1½ teaspoons Italian seasoning

1 bay leaf

2 tablespoons chopped fresh flat-leaf parsley

NOTE

For a grain-free soup, substitute 1 pound of peeled, diced russet potatoes for the rice.

Seitan Stew with Red Wine and Herbs

SERVES 4 TO 6

1 pound seitan (page 151)

¼ teaspoon fine sea salt

½ teaspoon freshly ground black pepper

1 tablespoon avocado oil or other neutral oil

1 yellow onion, diced

4 cloves garlic, minced

½ cup red wine

1 teaspoon chopped fresh rosemary

1 teaspoon fresh thyme leaves

1 teaspoon chopped fresh sage leaves

1 cup low-sodium vegetable broth (page 152)

2 teaspoons Dijon mustard

8 ounces (4 medium) carrots, peeled and sliced into 1-inch rounds

1 large rutabaga (about 1-pound), peeled and cut into 1-inch pieces

1 pound (about 3) waxy potatoes, cut into 1-inch pieces

1 tablespoon tomato paste

I got so excited the first time I made seitan in the Instant Pot. When you make this wheat gluten product yourself, you can shape it any way you like, including into bite-sized pieces that work perfectly in this hearty stew.

———————

Blot the seitan dry between paper towels. Sprinkle with the salt and pepper.

Select the **Sauté** setting on the Instant Pot, add the oil, and heat for 2 minutes. Swirl the oil around to cover the bottom of the pot, then add the seitan and let sear for 4 minutes, until golden brown. Use a thin, flexible spatula to unstick the seitan and flip it, then let it sear for 3 minutes more. Use the spatula to unstick the pieces once more, then transfer the seitan to a dish and set aside. There may be a lot of browned seitan bits stuck to the bottom of the pot—this is normal.

Add the onion and garlic to the pot and sauté for 4 minutes, until the onion softens. Stir in the wine, using a wooden spoon to nudge loose any browned bits from the bottom of the pot. Let the wine simmer until it has mostly evaporated, about 4 minutes. Add the herbs and sauté 1 minute more. Add the broth and mustard and stir to dissolve, scraping up any stuck-on bits from the bottom of the pot one last time. Bring the mixture up to a simmer (this will take about 1 minute), then stir in the seitan, carrots, rutabaga, and potatoes. Add the tomato paste on top. Do not stir.

Secure the lid and set the Pressure Release to **Sealing**. Press the **Cancel** button to reset the cooking program. Then select the **Meat/Stew** setting and set the cooking time for 4 minutes at high pressure. (The pot will take about 15 minutes to come up to pressure before the cooking program begins.)

When the cooking program ends, perform a quick pressure release by moving the Pressure Release to **Venting**. Open the pot and gently stir the stew to incorporate the tomato paste and make sure everything is coated with the cooking liquid.

Ladle the stew into bowls and serve hot.

Tomato Soup with Welsh Rarebit Toasties

Freshly made tomato soup tastes so much better than anything you can buy. Using good-quality canned tomatoes (San Marzano, if you can find them) is important, since they are the main flavor in the soup. The real star of this show might be the toasties that go alongside, though. The rarebit sauce is broiled on top of crusty bread for an open-faced, "cheesy" delight.

————————

To make the soup: Select the **Sauté** setting on the Instant Pot, add the oil, and heat for 1 minute. Add the onion, carrots, garlic, and salt and sauté for 5 minutes, until the onion softens but is not browned. Add the tomatoes and their liquid, broth, rice, and Italian seasoning. Leave the tomatoes whole.

Secure the lid and set the Pressure Release to **Sealing**. Press the **Cancel** button to reset the cooking program. Then select the **Soup/Broth** setting and set the cooking time for 5 minutes at high pressure. (The pot will take about 15 minutes to come up to pressure before the cooking program begins.)

While the soup is cooking, make the topping for the toasties: In a blender, combine the cashews, water, garlic, nutritional yeast, mustard, Worcestershire, tomato paste, salt, and cayenne. Blend at high speed for about 1 minute, until smooth, scraping down the sides of the blender halfway through, if necessary. Taste for seasoning, adding salt if needed.

When the cooking program ends, let the pressure release naturally for 10 minutes, then move the Pressure Release to **Venting** to release any remaining steam.

continued

SERVES 4 TO 6

SOUP

2 tablespoons extra-virgin olive oil

1 yellow onion, diced

2 carrots, peeled and diced

1 clove garlic, minced

¼ teaspoon fine sea salt, plus more as needed

1 (28-ounce) can whole peeled tomatoes

2 cups low-sodium vegetable broth (page 152)

¼ cup medium- or long-grain white rice

1½ teaspoons Italian seasoning

TOASTIES

1 cup raw cashews, soaked in water for 2 hours at room temperature, or up to overnight in the refrigerator, and drained

¼ cup water

1 clove garlic, minced

2 tablespoons nutritional yeast

1½ tablespoons prepared yellow mustard

1 tablespoon vegan Worcestershire sauce

1 tablespoon tomato paste

Tomato Soup with Welsh Rarebit Toasties, continued

½ teaspoon fine sea salt,
plus more as needed

¼ teaspoon cayenne
pepper

6 (1-inch) slices French or
sourdough bâtard

Freshly ground black
pepper for serving

While the pressure is releasing, assemble the toasties: Spread a few tablespoons of the blended mixture on each slice of bread. Toast in a toaster oven or under a broiler for 3 to 5 minutes, until the topping is lightly browned.

Open the pot and use an immersion blender to puree the soup until smooth. Taste and adjust the seasoning with salt, if needed.

Ladle the soup into mugs or bowls, sprinkle with a few grinds of pepper, and serve piping hot, with the toasties on the side.

Hot and Sour Soup

SERVES 6 TO 8

2 tablespoons avocado oil or other neutral oil

1-inch knob fresh ginger, peeled and finely grated

3 cloves garlic, minced

1 teaspoon ground white pepper 6 cups mushroom broth (page 153)

8 ounces (about 12 medium) cremini or button mushrooms, sliced

8 dried shiitake mushrooms, rehydrated in boiling water for 30 minutes

1 (8-ounce) can sliced bamboo shoots, rinsed and drained

1 (14-ounce) block firm tofu, drained

2 tablespoons cornstarch

2 tablespoons rice vinegar

1 tablespoon water

1 tablespoon soy sauce, tamari, or coconut aminos

1 tablespoon turbinado or organic cane sugar

4 green onions, white and tender green parts, thinly sliced

¼ cup chopped fresh cilantro

Don't you just love being able to make take out favorites at home in true vegan style? This hot and sour soup is a hearty one, packed with lots of mushrooms and tofu. I especially like to make it when I'm feeling under the weather—all of that spicy ginger and white pepper really helps to clear my head.

———————————

Select the **Sauté** setting on the Instant Pot, add 1 tablespoon of the oil, the ginger, and garlic, and heat for about 2 minutes, until the mixture is bubbling and fragrant but not browned. Add the white pepper and sauté for about 1 minute more. Add the broth, cremini and shiitake mushrooms, and bamboo shoots and stir to combine, using a wooden spoon to nudge loose any browned bits from the bottom of the pot.

Secure the lid and set the Pressure Release to **Sealing**. Press the **Cancel** button to reset the cooking program. Then select the **Soup/Broth** setting and set the cooking time for 5 minutes at high pressure. (The pot will take about 15 minutes to come up to pressure before the cooking program begins.)

While the soup cooks, cut the tofu into ½-inch slices. Sandwich the slices in a single layer between double layers of paper towels or a folded kitchen towel and press firmly to wick away as much moisture as possible. Cut the slices into ½-inch cubes.

In a large nonstick skillet over medium-high heat, warm the remaining 1 tablespoon oil. Add the tofu in a single layer and cook without stirring for about 3 minutes, or until lightly browned. Using a spatula, turn the cubes over and cook for about 3 minutes more, until browned on the other side. Remove from the heat and set aside.

In a small bowl, combine the cornstarch, vinegar, water, soy sauce, and sugar and stir to combine (the sugar may not dissolve completely). Set aside.

When the cooking program ends, let the pressure release naturally for 15 minutes, then move the Pressure Release to **Venting** to release any remaining steam. Open the pot, then stir in the seared tofu. Stir the cornstarch mixture to recombine, then stir it into the soup. Press the **Cancel** button to reset the cooking program. Then select the **Sauté** setting. Bring the soup to a simmer and cook for about 4 minutes, stirring occasionally, until the soup thickens. Press the **Cancel** button to turn off the pot, then stir in the green onions and cilantro.

Ladle the soup into bowls and serve piping hot.

Miso Soup with Shiitakes and Snap Peas

Miso soup doesn't require cooking under pressure—this version cooks entirely on the Instant Pot's Sauté setting and comes together in about 15 minutes. Freshly grated garlic and ginger give the soup depth of flavor, so you won't miss the traditional bonito flakes. Serve as a first course for a Japanese-inspired meal, or sip as a mid-day snack.

Select the **Sauté** setting on the Instant Pot, add the oil, garlic, and ginger, and heat for 2 minutes, until bubbling. Add the mushrooms and sauté for 1 minute, until they begin to wilt and the ginger and garlic begin to brown on the bottom of the pot. Stir in the water and peas, using a wooden spoon to nudge loose any browned bits from the bottom of the pot. Cover with the glass lid and let come up to a simmer (this will take about 8 minutes).

Remove the lid and press the **Cancel** button to turn off the pot.

Put the miso paste in a small bowl. Ladle ¼ cup of the liquid from the pot into the bowl, then mash the miso against the side of the bowl and stir until it is fully dissolved. Add the miso mixture and the green onions to the pot and stir to combine.

Ladle the soup into bowls and serve piping hot.

**SERVES 4
AS A FIRST COURSE**

1 teaspoon avocado oil or other neutral oil

2 cloves garlic, finely grated

½-inch knob ginger, peeled and finely grated

4 ounces fresh shiitake mushrooms, stems removed, thinly sliced

4 cups water

2 cups (8 ounces) sugar snap peas, cut into ½-inch pieces

¼ cup white miso paste

2 green onions, white and tender green parts, thinly sliced

NOTE

Shiitakes and snap peas are a light option for spring and summer, but you can substitute other seasonal vegetables, if you like. Cremini or button mushrooms, carrots, asparagus, and corn kernels are all good options. Just dice or slice vegetables small so they only take a few minutes to cook through. You can also add cubed soft tofu, nori, or dried wakame seaweed.

Double Lentil Soup with Gremolata

SERVES 4 TO 6

SOUP

2 tablespoons extra-virgin olive oil, plus more for serving

1 large yellow onion, diced

2 carrots, peeled and diced

2 celery stalks, diced

2 cloves garlic, minced

1 teaspoon fine sea salt, plus more as needed

½ cup French green (Puy) lentils

½ cup beluga lentils

4 cups low-sodium vegetable broth (page 152)

2 tablespoons fresh lemon juice

GREMOLATA

1 cup loosely packed fresh flat-leaf parsley leaves

1 clove garlic, peeled

Finely grated zest of 1 lemon

Crusty bread for serving

Different types of lentils lend slightly different textures to soup. Experiment to figure out what you like best. Red lentils will break down completely, French green (Puy) and beluga lentils will mostly retain their shape, and regular green or brown lentils fall somewhere in between. Here, I've used French green and beluga lentils, but you really can use whatever kind you have on hand. Gremolata, a mixture of chopped parsley, garlic, and lemon zest, is added at the end of cooking for a hit of fresh flavor.

———————————

To make the soup: Select the **Sauté** setting on the Instant Pot, add the oil, and heat for 1 minute. Add the onion, carrots, celery, garlic, and salt and sauté for about 5 minutes, until the onion softens. Add the lentils and broth and stir to combine.

Secure the lid and set the Pressure Release to **Sealing**. Press the **Cancel** button to reset the cooking program. Then select the **Soup/Broth** setting and set the cooking time for 15 minutes at high pressure. (The pot will take about 10 minutes to come up to pressure before the cooking program begins.)

While the soup is cooking, make the gremolata: Pile the parsley onto a cutting board, along with the garlic. Chop them together until the parsley is finely chopped and there are no large bits of garlic. Add the lemon zest and chop a little more, until the mixture is combined.

When the cooking program ends, let the pressure release naturally for 10 minutes, then move the Pressure Release to **Venting** to release any remaining steam. Open the pot, then stir in the gremolata and lemon juice. Taste and adjust the seasoning with salt, if needed.

Ladle the soup into bowls and drizzle with oil. Serve piping hot, with crusty bread alongside.

Split Pea Soup with Old Bay Croutons

Split pea soup is the perfect recipe to throw together in the Instant Pot in the morning—you can let the pressure release naturally and leave the pot on its default Keep Warm setting until it's time to serve the soup for lunch or dinner. Crunchy, Old Bay–spiced croutons take this soup from basic to special with only a few minutes of extra prep.

———————

To make the soup: Select the **Sauté** setting on the Instant Pot, add the oil, and heat for 1 minute. Add the onion, carrots, and celery and sauté for 5 minutes, until the onion softens. Add the Old Bay, smoked paprika, pepper, split peas, broth, water, and bay leaf. Stir to combine.

Secure the lid and set the Pressure Release to **Sealing**. Press the **Cancel** button to reset the cooking program. Then select the **Manual** or **Pressure Cook** setting and set the cooking time for 20 minutes at high pressure. (The pot will take about 25 minutes to come up to pressure before the cooking program begins.)

When the cooking program ends, let the pressure release naturally (this will take about 45 minutes). Open the pot, then remove and discard the bay leaf.

When you're ready to serve the soup, make the croutons: In a bowl, toss the cubed bread with the oil and Old Bay until the bread is evenly coated. Spread out the bread in an even layer on a foil-lined baking sheet, and toast in a toaster oven or under a broiler for about 3–5 minutes, until lightly browned.

Ladle the soup into bowls and serve piping hot, with the croutons and smoked paprika sprinkled on top and a drizzle of oil.

SERVES 8

SOUP

2 tablespoons extra-virgin olive oil, plus more for serving

1 yellow onion, diced

2 carrots, peeled and diced

2 celery stalks, diced

1 tablespoon Old Bay seasoning

1 teaspoon smoked paprika

½ teaspoon freshly ground black pepper

2⅓ cups (1 pound) green split peas

4 cups low-sodium vegetable broth (page 152)

4 cups water

1 bay leaf

CROUTONS

4 slices crusty bread, cut into ½-inch cubes

2 tablespoons extra-virgin olive oil

1 teaspoon Old Bay seasoning

Smoked paprika for serving

Cassoulet with Garlic Sausages

SERVES 8

Homemade sausages and fancy flageolet beans get a topping of herbed bread crumbs in this impressive and hearty stew. It's a tummy-warmer of a dish, perfect for chilly winter nights. Think of it as an elevated take on franks and beans, with a dash of French flair. Serve it with glasses of red wine.

BEANS

2 tablespoons extra-virgin olive oil

2 cloves garlic, minced

1 yellow onion, diced

2 stalks celery, diced

1 large carrot, diced

1 teaspoon dried thyme

1 bay leaf

2 cups (13½ ounces) dried flageolet beans

4 cups low-sodium vegetable broth (page 152)

2 tablespoons tomato paste

SAUSAGES

2 tablespoons nutritional yeast

2 tablespoons extra-virgin olive oil

1 tablespoon tomato paste

2 cloves garlic, minced

1½ teaspoons herbes de Provence

¾ teaspoon fine sea salt

½ teaspoon freshly ground black pepper

1 cup vital wheat gluten

¾ cup low-sodium vegetable broth (page 152)

To make the beans: Select the **Sauté** setting on the Instant Pot, add the oil and garlic, and heat for 2 minutes, until the garlic is bubbling. Add the onion, celery, and carrot, and sauté for 5 minutes, until the onion softens. Add the thyme and bay leaf and sauté for 1 minute more. Stir in the beans and broth, using a wooden spoon to nudge loose any browned bits from the bottom of the pot.

Secure the lid and set the Pressure Release to **Sealing**. Press the **Cancel** button to reset the cooking program. Then select the **Manual, Pressure Cook**, or **Bean/Chili** setting and set the cooking time for 25 minutes at high pressure. (The pot will take about 10 minutes to come up to pressure before the cooking program begins.)

When the cooking program ends, let the pressure release naturally (this will take about 30 minutes). Open the pot and discard the bay leaf. Press the **Cancel** button to turn off the pot. Wearing heat-resistant mitts, lift the inner pot out of the Instant Pot housing. Use a slotted spoon to measure out ¾ cup beans and set aside. To the inner pot, add the tomato paste and stir to combine. Transfer the remaining beans and their liquid to an 8 by 10-inch baking dish, cover the dish, and set aside. Rinse out the inner pot and return it to the housing.

To make the sausages: In a food processor, combine the reserved ¾ cup beans with the nutritional yeast, 1 tablespoon of the oil, tomato paste, garlic, herbes de Provence, salt, and pepper. Process in about ten 1-second pulses until fairly smooth, scraping down the sides of the container, if necessary. Add the wheat gluten and broth and pulse about 15 more times, until a ball of dough forms.

continued

Cassoulet with Garlic Sausages, continued

Turn the dough out onto a work surface and divide it into four even pieces. Roll a piece into a 6-inch log, then place it on top of an 8-inch square of parchment paper. Roll the log in the parchment and tie the ends with kitchen twine. Repeat with the remaining dough to make three more sausages.

Pour 1 cup water into the Instant Pot and place the wire metal steam rack inside. Place the sausages in a single layer on the rack. Secure the lid and set the Pressure Release to **Sealing,** then select the **Steam** setting and set the cooking time for 20 minutes at high pressure. (The pot will take about 5 minutes to come up to pressure before the cooking program begins.)

While the sausages are steaming, make the bread crumb topping: In a bowl, stir together the bread crumbs, parsley, and oil. Set aside.

When the cooking program ends, let the pressure release naturally for 10 minutes, then move the Pressure Release to **Venting** to release any remaining steam. Wearing heat-resistant mitts, grasp the handles of the steam rack and lift the sausages out of the pot. Let the sausages cool for 5 minutes, then transfer to a cutting board. Remove the parchment paper, taking care not to get burned from the steam. Slice the sausages in half lengthwise, then into ½-inch-thick pieces.

Preheat the oven to 375°F.

Heat the remaining 1 tablespoon of oil in a nonstick skillet over medium heat. Add the sausages and sear for 5 minutes, turning the pieces occasionally so they are lightly browned all over. Uncover the baking dish, add the sausages, and use a spoon to poke them down into the beans.

Sprinkle the bread crumb topping evenly over the beans and sausages. Bake the cassoulet, uncovered, for 30 to 35 minutes, until the bread crumbs are golden brown and the beans are heated through and bubbling. Scoop portions onto plates and serve warm.

BREAD CRUMB TOPPING

¾ cup panko bread crumbs

2 tablespoons chopped fresh flat-leaf parsley

1 tablespoon extra-virgin olive oil

NOTES

Use this whole recipe for a showstopper of a main dish, or substitute ¾ cup canned beans to skip the cassoulet and just make the garlic sausages.

For a faster cassoulet, substitute store-bought vegan sausages, such as Field Roast brand.

Winter Vegetable Chili

SERVES 4 TO 6

3 tablespoons extra-virgin olive oil

2 cloves garlic, minced

2 leeks, white and tender green parts, halved lengthwise and thinly sliced

2 jalapeño chiles, seeded and diced

1 teaspoon fine sea salt, plus more as needed

1 canned chipotle chile in adobo sauce, minced

3 tablespoons chili powder

1 cup low-sodium vegetable broth (page 152)

2 carrots, peeled and diced

1½ cups cooked black beans (page 144), or 1 (15-ounce) can beans, rinsed and drained

1 (1-pound) delicata squash, seeded and diced

1 (14½-ounce) can diced fire-roasted tomatoes

Chopped fresh cilantro for serving

When it's cold out, I pack my pot of chili with hearty vegetables like leeks, carrots, and winter squash. Delicata squash holds up particularly well, and it's easy to prep since there's no peeling required. You can play around with the ingredients—use any kind of beans you like, sub in serranos for jalapeños if you want even more spice, or use an onion instead of the leeks if that's what you have on hand. With vegan chili, anything goes!

Select the **Sauté** setting on the Instant Pot, add the oil and garlic, and heat for 2 minutes, until the garlic is bubbling. Add the leeks, jalapeños, and salt and sauté for 5 minutes, until the leeks are wilted and beginning to release their moisture. Add the chipotle chile and chili powder and sauté for 1 minute more. Stir in the broth, using a wooden spoon to nudge loose any browned bits from the bottom of the pot. In fairly even layers, add the carrots to the pot, followed by the beans and the squash. Pour the tomatoes and their liquid over the top. Do not stir.

Secure the lid and set the Pressure Release to **Sealing**. Press the **Cancel** button to reset the cooking program. Then select the **Manual** or **Pressure Cook** setting and set the cooking time for 5 minutes at high pressure. (The pot will take about 15 minutes to come up to pressure before the cooking program begins.)

When the cooking program ends, perform a quick pressure release by moving the Pressure Release to **Venting**. Open the pot, stir everything together, then taste the chili and adjust the seasoning with salt, if needed.

Ladle the chili into bowls and sprinkle with cilantro. Serve piping hot.

Summer Vegetable Chili

This chili is on the lighter side, and it's good in the summertime, or anytime you want a bit of summery flavor. Poblano and jalapeño chiles, zucchini, corn, and tomatoes make up the vegetables, and pinto or peruano beans add the hit of heartiness that every chili needs. Serve it on its own, or over rice for a more filling meal.

———————

Select the **Sauté** setting on the Instant Pot, add the oil, and heat for 1 minute. Add the poblano and jalapeño chiles, onion, celery, garlic, and salt, and sauté for about 5 minutes, until the vegetables soften. Add the chili powder, oregano, cumin, and cayenne and sauté for about 1 minute more. Add the zucchini, corn, beans, and broth and stir to combine. Pour the tomatoes and their liquid over the top. Do not stir.

Secure the lid and set the Pressure Release to **Sealing**. Press the **Cancel** button to reset the cooking program. Then select the **Manual** or **Pressure Cook** setting and set the cooking time for 5 minutes at high pressure. (The pot will take about 15 minutes to come up to pressure before the cooking program begins.)

When the cooking program ends, perform a quick pressure release by moving the Pressure Release to **Venting**. Open the pot, stir everything together then taste the chili and adjust the seasoning with salt, if needed.

Ladle the chili into bowls and sprinkle with cilantro and green onions. Serve piping hot.

SERVES 6

2 tablespoons extra-virgin olive oil

1 poblano chile or green bell pepper, seeded and diced

1 jalapeño chile, seeded and diced

1 yellow onion, diced

1 celery stalk, diced

2 cloves garlic, minced

½ teaspoon fine sea salt, plus more as needed

2 tablespoons chili powder

1 teaspoon dried oregano

½ teaspoon ground cumin

¼ teaspoon cayenne pepper

2 zucchini, diced

1 (12-ounce) bag frozen corn, or kernels cut from 3 ears fresh corn

1½ cups cooked pinto or peruano beans (page 144), or 1 (15-ounce) can beans, rinsed and drained

1 cup low-sodium vegetable broth (page 152)

1 (14½-ounce) can diced fire-roasted tomatoes

¼ cup chopped fresh cilantro

2 green onions, white and tender green parts, thinly sliced

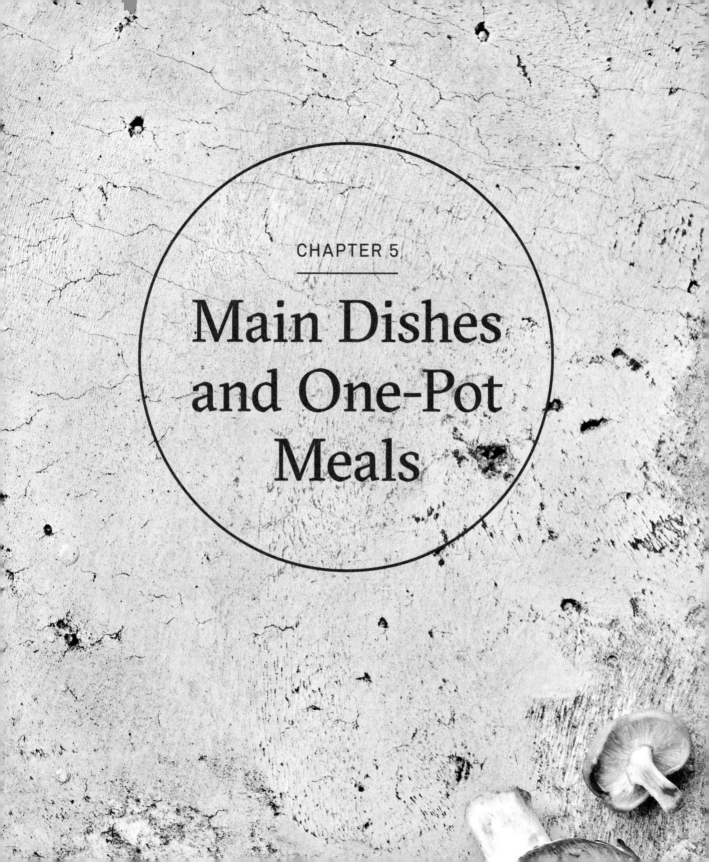

CHAPTER 5

Main Dishes and One-Pot Meals

Palak Tofu with Jeera Rice

SERVES 4

RICE

1 cup basmati rice, rinsed and drained

1 cup water

½ teaspoon whole cumin seeds

¼ teaspoon fine sea salt

PALAK TOFU

1 (14-ounce) block extra-firm tofu, drained

5 tablespoons coconut oil or other oil with a high smoke point

1 yellow onion, diced

1-inch knob fresh ginger, peeled and minced

3 cloves garlic, minced

1 teaspoon fine sea salt, plus more as needed

½ teaspoon freshly ground black pepper

¼ teaspoon cayenne pepper

1 (16-ounce) bag frozen chopped spinach

⅓ cup water

1 (14½-ounce) can diced fire roasted tomatoes

¼ cup coconut milk or coconut cream

2 teaspoons garam masala

Did you know you can cook a bowl of rice on top of another dish, right in the same pot? This style of pot-in-pot cooking (or bowl-in-pot, as the case may be) is one of my favorite weeknight tricks. Cumin-studded rice steams atop a pot full of hearty spiced tofu. Extra-firm tofu has a texture and mild flavor that's similar to Indian paneer, so it's the perfect stand-in for a veganized version.

———————

To make the rice: In a 1½-quart stainless-steel bowl, stir together the rice, water, cumin seeds, and salt. Set aside.

To make the palak tofu: Cut the tofu into ½-inch slices. Sandwich the slices in a single layer between double layers of paper towels or a folded kitchen towel and press firmly to wick away as much moisture as possible. Cut the slices into ½-inch cubes.

Select the high **Sauté** setting on the Instant Pot, add 4 tablespoons of the coconut oil, and melt. Add the onion and sauté for about 10 minutes, until it begins to brown.

Meanwhile, warm the remaining 1 tablespoon coconut oil in a large nonstick skillet over medium-high heat. Add the tofu in a single layer and cook without stirring for about 3 minutes, or until lightly browned. Using a spatula, turn the cubes over and cook for about 3 minutes more, until browned on the other side. Remove from the heat and set aside.

When the onion is browned, add the ginger and garlic and sauté for about 2 minutes, until the garlic is fragrant but not browned. Add the reserved tofu, salt, black pepper, and cayenne and gently stir to combine, taking care not to break up the tofu. Gently stir in the spinach. Pour the water and the tomatoes and their liquid over the top in an even layer but do not stir.

Place a tall steam rack in the pot, making sure all of its legs rest firmly on the bottom of the pot. Place the bowl of rice on the rack.

Secure the lid and set the Pressure Release to **Sealing**. Press the **Cancel** button to reset the cooking program. Then select the **Manual** or **Pressure Cook** setting and set the cooking time for 10 minutes at low pressure. (The pot will take about 15 minutes to come up to pressure before the cooking program begins.)

When the cooking program ends, let the pressure release naturally for 10 minutes, then move the Pressure Release to **Venting** to release any remaining steam. Open the pot and, wearing heatproof mitts, remove the bowl of rice and the steam rack. Use a fork to fluff the rice.

Add the coconut milk and garam masala to the pot and stir to combine. Taste for seasoning and add salt, if needed.

Ladle the palak tofu onto serving plates or into bowls. Serve piping hot, with the rice.

Massaman Curry with Tofu and Kabocha Squash

1 (14-ounce) block firm tofu, drained

1 tablespoon coconut oil

1 large yellow onion, cut into 1-inch pieces

½ cup coconut cream

¼ cup Massaman curry paste

1 cup low-sodium vegetable broth (page 152)

1 (1½-pound) kabocha squash, seeded and cut into 1-inch cubes

1 cup coconut milk

1 cup loosely packed fresh Thai basil leaves

Hot steamed rice (page 146) for serving

NOTE

If you like, you can brown the tofu while the squash is cooking in the Instant Pot. Melt 1 tablespoon of coconut oil in a nonstick skillet over medium heat and sear the tofu for 3 minutes per side (6 minutes total), until it is lightly browned. Remove from the heat and set aside until it is time to add the tofu to the pot with the coconut milk.

If you're a chili head, you'll appreciate the generous amount of Massaman curry paste used in this Thai-style dish—it's not shy on spice. When buying your curry paste, do check the ingredients to make sure it is vegan. Aroy-D brand is a great choice. Their coconut milk is excellent and consistent in quality, too.

Cut the tofu into ½-inch slices. Sandwich the slices in a single layer between double layers of paper towels or a folded kitchen towel and press firmly to wick away as much moisture as possible. Cut the slices into ½-inch cubes. Set aside.

Select the high **Sauté** setting on the Instant Pot, add the coconut oil, and melt. Add the onion and sauté for 4 minutes, until the onion starts to brown. Add the coconut cream and curry paste and sauté for 2 minutes more, until bubbling and fragrant. Stir in the broth, using a wooden spoon to nudge loose any browned bits from the pot bottom, then add the squash in a single layer.

Secure the lid and set the Pressure Release to **Sealing**. Press the **Cancel** button to reset the cooking program. Then select the **Manual** or **Pressure Cook** setting and set the cooking time for 1 minute at low pressure. (The pot will take about 10 minutes to come up to pressure before the cooking program begins.)

When the cooking program ends, perform a quick pressure release by moving the Pressure Release to **Venting**. Open the pot and stir in the coconut milk, then add the tofu. Press the **Cancel** button to reset the cooking program. Then select the **Sauté** setting. Let the curry come up to a simmer and cook for 2 minutes, stirring occasionally and gently, being careful not to break up the tofu. Press the **Cancel** button to turn off the pot. Gently stir in the basil.

Ladle the curry into bowls. Serve piping hot with the rice on the side.

Enchilada Casserole with Chipotle Cashew Cream

SERVES 4 TO 6

ENCHILADA SAUCE

6 ancho chiles, stemmed and seeded

3 tablespoons extra-virgin olive oil

2 cloves garlic, minced

1 yellow onion, diced

1 teaspoon dried oregano

½ teaspoon ground cumin

1 (14½-ounce) can fire-roasted diced tomatoes

¾ cup water

1 teaspoon fine sea salt

1½ cups frozen corn kernels, thawed

1 large (8-ounce) zucchini, diced small

1½ cups cooked black beans (page 144), or 1 (15-ounce) can black beans, rinsed and drained

4 tablespoons chopped fresh cilantro, divided

5 extra-large corn tortillas

Chipotle cashew cream (page 157) for serving

Homemade enchilada sauce and chipotle cashew cream are worth the effort for this Mexican-inspired dish. Layered like a lasagna, this casserole is so much easier to assemble than a pan full of rolled enchiladas. Mission Brand Super Size corn tortillas fit perfectly inside a Pyrex 7-cup round dish, but if you can't find them, just cut up smaller tortillas and arrange them in even layers.

———————————

To make the enchilada sauce: Put the chiles in a heatproof bowl and pour 2 cups boiling water over them. Let soak for about 20 minutes, until the chiles are softened.

While the chiles are soaking, select the **Sauté** setting on the Instant Pot, add the oil and garlic, and heat for 2 minutes, until the garlic is bubbling. Add the onion and sauté for 5 minutes, until softened. Add the oregano and cumin and sauté for 1 minute more. Press the **Cancel** button to turn off the pot. Add the tomatoes and their liquid and stir, using a wooden spoon to nudge loose any browned bits from the bottom of the pot.

Wearing heat-resistant mitts, lift the inner pot out of the housing and transfer the sautéed mixture to a blender. Add the water and salt. Drain the soaked chiles and add them as well. Blend at high speed for 1 minute, until smooth.

Rinse out the inner pot and return it to the housing. Pour 1 cup water into the Instant Pot.

In a mixing bowl, combine the corn, zucchini, beans, and 2 tablespoons of the cilantro.

Ladle ¼ cup of the sauce into a 7-cup round heatproof glass container and spread it out in an even layer. Place a tortilla on top, then sprinkle in 1 heaping cup of the corn mixture. Pour on ½ cup sauce and spread it out evenly over the vegetables. Repeat layers of tortilla, vegetables, and sauce three more times, then add one more tortilla on top.

Cover the container tightly with aluminum foil and place it on top of a long-handled silicone steam rack. Grasping the arms of the rack, lower it into the Instant Pot.

Secure the lid and set the Pressure Release to **Sealing**. Select the **Steam** setting and set the cooking time for 40 minutes at high pressure. (The pot will take about 10 minutes to come up to pressure before the cooking program begins.)

When the cooking program ends, let the pressure release naturally for 10 minutes, then move the Pressure Release to **Venting** to release any remaining steam. Open the pot and, wearing heat-resistant mitts, grab the handles of the steam rack and lift the casserole out of the pot. Uncover the casserole, taking care not to get burned by the steam.

Use a serving spoon to scoop portions of the casserole into serving bowls or onto plates. Spoon some of the chipotle cashew cream on top, sprinkle with the remaining chopped cilantro, and serve warm.

NOTE

You'll have some leftover enchilada sauce, which also makes a great dip for chips. Leftover enchilada sauce keeps well refrigerated in an airtight container for up to 1 week, or frozen for up to 3 months.

Hoppin' John Burgers

Black-eyed peas and rice are the main ingredients in the Southern dish Hoppin' John, and they make a great base for veggie burgers, too. The burgers are spiced with Old Bay and a touch of cayenne, with chopped walnuts mixed in for a little more texture. The burger mixture is cooked in the Instant Pot, then shaped into patties and baked in the oven.

Select the **Sauté** setting on the Instant Pot, add the oil and garlic, and heat for 2 minutes, until the garlic is bubbling but not browned. Add the onion and mushrooms and sauté for 5 minutes, until the onion softens and the mushrooms wilt and give up their liquid. Add the Old Bay, black pepper, and cayenne, and sauté for 1 more minute.

Stir in the broth, black-eyed peas, and rice, using a wooden spoon to nudge loose any browned bits from the bottom of the pot. Scrape down any grains of rice stuck to the sides of the pot, making sure the rice and beans are fully submerged in the broth. Add the tomato paste in a dollop on top. Do not stir.

Secure the lid and set the Pressure Release to **Sealing**. Press the **Cancel** button to reset the cooking program. Then select the **Manual, Pressure Cook,** or **Bean/Chili** setting and set the cooking time for 25 minutes at high pressure. (The pot will take about 5 minutes to come up to pressure before the cooking program begins.)

When the cooking program ends, let the pressure release naturally for 10 minutes, then move the Pressure Release to **Venting** to release any remaining steam. Open the pot and, wearing heat-resistant mitts, lift out the inner pot. Add the carrot, bread crumbs, and walnuts and stir to combine. Use a potato masher to mash up some of the beans if you want a denser, more cohesive texture. Let the mixture stand for 10 minutes to firm up and cool down a bit.

continued

3 tablespoons extra-virgin olive oil

3 cloves garlic, minced

1 small yellow onion, finely chopped

4 ounces (about 6 medium) cremini or button mushrooms, finely chopped

2 teaspoons Old Bay seasoning

½ teaspoon freshly ground black pepper

¼ teaspoon cayenne pepper

2 cups low-sodium vegetable broth (page 152)

¾ cup (4½ ounces) dried black-eyed peas

¾ cup medium- or long-grain brown rice

1 tablespoon tomato paste

1 large carrot, finely shredded (use a coarse Microplane)

¾ cup panko bread crumbs

½ cup walnut halves and pieces, toasted and chopped

8 hamburger buns

Iceberg lettuce, sliced tomatoes, sliced sweet onions, ketchup, mustard, and pickle chips for serving

Hoppin' John Burgers, continued

NOTES

Vegan hamburger bun brands include Rudi's Organic Bakery and Nature's Own 100% Whole Wheat.

For thicker, restaurant-style burgers, portion out five ¾-cup scoops of the mixture onto the baking sheet instead of eight ½-cup scoops. Keep the baking time the same.

While the burger mixture is cooling, preheat the oven to 375°F. Line a baking sheet with parchment paper or a silicone mat and grease it lightly with olive oil or nonstick cooking spray.

Using a ½-cup measure, portion the burger mixture out onto the baking sheet to make eight burgers. Use your fingertips to pat the burgers out into 4-inch patties, rinsing your hands between burgers if they become sticky.

Bake the burgers for 20 minutes, until they are lightly browned and crispy on the outside. In the last few minutes that the burgers are baking, toast the hamburger buns.

Use a thin, flexible spatula to transfer the burgers to the toasted buns. Serve warm, with lettuce, tomatoes, onions, ketchup, mustard, and pickles.

Jackfruit and Black Bean Burritos

You'll want to buy jackfruit canned in brine, which is known as green, or unripe. Here, it's prepared as a filling for burritos, and pot-in-pot cooking allows you to cook your jackfruit and warm up your black beans all at the same time.

———————

Put the beans in a 1½-quart stainless-steel bowl. Rinse the jackfruit under running water. Drain well, then transfer to a cutting board. Cut off and thinly slice the tougher cores and seeds, then pull the stringy part of the jackfruit into shreds.

Select the **Sauté** setting on the Instant Pot, add the oil and garlic, and heat for 2 minutes, until the garlic is bubbling but not browned. Add the onion and sauté for 5 minutes, until softened and just beginning to brown. Stir in the chili powder, salt, orange juice, lime juice, and soy sauce, using a wooden spoon to nudge loose any browned bits from the bottom of the pot. Stir in the jackfruit, then use a spoon to arrange it in an even layer. Add the chipotle and tomato paste in dollops on top of the jackfruit; do not stir them in. Place the tall steam rack in the pot, making sure all of the legs rest firmly on the bottom, and place the bowl of beans on top of the rack.

Secure the lid and set the Pressure Release to **Sealing**. Press **Cancel** to reset the cooking program. Then select the **Manual** or **Pressure Cook** setting and set the cooking time for 5 minutes at high pressure. (The pot will take about 10 minutes to come up to pressure before the cooking program begins.)

Let the pressure release naturally for 5 minutes, then move the Pressure Release to **Venting** to release any remaining steam. Open the pot and, wearing heat-resistant mitts, remove the bowl of beans and the steam rack. Stir the jackfruit mixture to incorporate the chipotle and tomato paste.

Place each warmed tortilla on top of a 12-inch square of aluminum foil. Use a slotted spoon to spoon the jackfruit onto the bottom third of the tortillas, then spoon on the black beans, rice, lettuce, and sour cream. Tucking in the sides of the tortillas, roll tightly from the bottom to form burritos. Wrap the burritos with the aluminum foil and serve warm.

SERVES 4

1½ cups cooked black beans (page 144), or 1 (15-ounce) can beans, rinsed and drained

2 (20-ounce) cans green jackfruit, packed in brine

2 tablespoons extra-virgin olive oil

4 cloves garlic, minced

1 yellow onion, diced

2 tablespoons chili powder

½ teaspoon fine sea salt

¾ cup fresh orange juice

2 tablespoons fresh lime juice

1 tablespoon soy sauce, tamari, or coconut aminos

1 canned chipotle in adobo sauce, minced

1 tablespoon tomato paste

4 burrito-size flour tortillas, warmed

2 cups steamed rice (page 146) or Mexican-Style Rice (page 43)

2 cups shredded romaine lettuce

½ cup vegan sour cream or chipotle cashew cream (page 157)

NOTE

For a milder version, leave out the chipotle.

Bulgur-Stuffed Bell Peppers with Garlic Sauce

The herb-studded filling is cooked in the Instant Pot, and the peppers bake for just 35 minutes, so they stay firm and juicy. Serve each person a half pepper as a side dish or first course, or two halves for a main-dish portion.

———————

To make the peppers: Select the **Sauté** setting on the Instant Pot, add the oil and garlic, and heat for 2 minutes, until the garlic is bubbling. Add the onion and sauté for 4 minutes, until softened. Stir in the broth, using a wooden spoon to nudge loose any browned bits from the bottom of the pot. Stir in the bulgur, scraping down the sides of the pot to make sure all of the grains are submerged in the liquid.

Secure the lid and set the Pressure Release to **Sealing**. Press the **Cancel** button to reset the cooking program. Then select the **Manual** or **Pressure Cook** setting and set the cooking time for 10 minutes at low pressure. (The pot will take about 5 minutes to come up to pressure before the cooking program begins.)

Preheat the oven to 375°F.

When the cooking program ends, let the pressure release naturally for 10 minutes, then move the Pressure Release to **Venting** to release any remaining steam. Open the pot and, wearing heat-resistant mitts, lift the inner pot out of the housing. Stir in the pine nuts, currants, 2 tablespoons of the parsley, and 1 tablespoon of the mint.

Place the pepper halves in a 9 by 13-inch baking dish. Spoon the bulgur mixture into the pepper halves, dividing it evenly among them (about ½ cup each). Cover the dish with aluminum foil. Bake for 35 minutes, until the peppers are cooked through.

While the peppers are baking, make the sauce: In a widemouthed pint jar, combine the cashews, oil, water, lemon juice, garlic, and salt. Use an immersion blender to blend the sauce until it is very smooth, about 2 minutes.

Use a serving spoon to transfer the peppers to plates. Serve warm, with the sauce spooned on top and sprinkled with the remaining parsley and mint.

SERVES 3 TO 6

PEPPERS

2 tablespoons extra-virgin olive oil

2 cloves garlic, minced

1 small yellow onion, diced

1½ cups low-sodium vegetable broth (page 152)

1 cup bulgur wheat

¼ cup pine nuts

¼ cup currants

3 tablespoons chopped fresh flat-leaf parsley

2 tablespoons chopped fresh mint

3 large bell peppers, cut in half lengthwise and seeded (stems left on)

SAUCE

½ cup raw cashews, soaked in water for 2 hours at room temperature, or up to overnight in the refrigerator, and drained

¼ cup avocado oil or grapeseed oil

¼ cup water

3 tablespoons fresh lemon juice

3 cloves garlic, minced

¾ teaspoon fine sea salt

Chickpea Salad Sandwiches with Aquafaba Mayonnaise

SERVES 4

1⅛ cups (8 ounces) dried chickpeas

1½ teaspoons fine sea salt, plus more as needed

3 cups water

1 tablespoon fresh lemon juice

⅛ teaspoon xanthan gum

½ cup grapeseed or avocado oil

½ small yellow onion, diced

2 celery stalks, diced

1 roasted bell pepper (half of a 12-ounce jar), diced

1 carrot, shredded

½ teaspoon freshly ground black pepper, plus more as needed

4 sandwich rolls, toasted

This recipe was inspired by the chickpea salad sandwiches on the menu at Farm House in Belmont, California. I knew I had to create a vegan version at home, since a chickpea salad bound with mayonnaise is practically begging to be made with aquafaba, the cooking water left behind when you boil a pot of chickpeas. This miracle ingredient is awesome for thickening and fluffing up the mayo, and it binds the salad together beautifully.

Add 4 cups of water, the chickpeas, and 1 teaspoon of the salt to the Instant Pot and stir to combine. Let soak for 10 to 12 hours, then drain in a colander. Or use the quick soak method: Secure the lid and set the Pressure Release to **Sealing**. Select the **Manual, Pressure Cook,** or **Bean/Chili** setting and set the cooking time for 2 minutes at high pressure. (The pot will take about 15 minutes to come up to pressure before the cooking program begins.)

Let the pressure release naturally for 30 minutes, then move the Pressure Release to **Venting** to release any remaining steam. Wearing heatproof mitts, lift out the inner pot and drain the beans in a colander. Return the inner pot to the housing. Return the beans to the pot. Add the 3 cups fresh water to the pot. Secure the lid and set the Pressure Release to **Sealing**. Select the **Manual, Pressure Cook,** or **Bean/Chili** setting and set the cooking time for 25 minutes at high pressure. (The pot will take about 10 minutes to come up to pressure before the cooking program begins.)

When the cooking program ends, let the pressure release naturally for 30 minutes, then move the Pressure Release to **Venting** to release any remaining steam. This time, you will reserve the cooking water for aquafaba. Place a colander over a bowl, drain the chickpeas in the colander, and pour all of the liquid (about 2 cups) back into the pot, leaving any sediment behind in the bowl. Set the chickpeas aside to cool.

Press the **Cancel** button to reset the cooking program. Then select the **Sauté** setting and let the cooking liquid reduce for about 15 minutes, until it has reduced by half, to 1 cup of liquid (this is your aquafaba). **Cancel** the cooking program to turn off the pot and, wearing heat-resistant mitts, lift the inner pot out of the housing.

Transfer the aquafaba to a jar and let it cool to room temperature. The aquafaba will keep, refrigerated, for up to 1 week.

In a widemouthed 1-pint jar, combine ¼ cup of the aquafaba, lemon juice, 1 tablespoon of the chickpeas, the remaining ½ teaspoon salt, xanthan gum, and oil. Plunge an immersion blender into the mixture, then blend until thick and smooth, about 1 minute. Leftover mayonnaise can be stored in an airtight container, refrigerated, for up to 5 days.

In a bowl, combine the remaining cooked chickpeas, ½ cup of the mayonnaise, the onion, celery, roasted bell pepper, carrot, and black pepper. Stir to mix all of the ingredients together evenly, then taste for seasoning, adding salt and/or black pepper, if needed.

Spoon the chickpea salad onto toasted sandwich rolls and serve immediately. Leftover salad can be stored in an airtight container, refrigerated, for up to 3 days.

NOTE

You can also use 2 (15-ounce) cans of chickpeas and their liquid to make this recipe. If using canned chickpeas, use their liquid for the mayo as-is, without reducing.

Mushroom-Stuffed Chard Rolls

SERVES 4 TO 6

ROLLS

2 bunches chard (about 1 pound; see Note), stems cut off at the base of the leaves and reserved

1 pound (about 24 medium) cremini mushrooms

1 yellow onion, peeled

2 zucchini, trimmed

2 carrots, peeled

¼ cup extra-virgin olive oil

1 teaspoon fine sea salt

1 teaspoon freshly ground black pepper

1 cup long-grain white rice

2 tablespoons tomato paste

SAUCE

1 (8-ounce) can tomato sauce

1½ cups water

2 tablespoons white wine vinegar

1 tablespoon vegan Worcestershire sauce

2 tablespoons turbinado or organic cane sugar

Cabbage rolls are an Eastern European comfort-food staple, but they are incredibly time-consuming and tedious to prepare, mostly due to the steps required to soften and separate the leaves from a whole head of cabbage. Steaming a bunch of chard is much easier, and much faster. This recipe is cooked in a stacked metal container (available through Instant Pot), so you end up with two pans of rolls. Serve them all at once, or set aside one pan and keep, refrigerated, for up to 3 days.

———————————

To make the rolls: Pour 1 cup water into the Instant Pot and place the wire metal steam rack in the pot. Stack the chard leaves on the rack, pressing them down gently so they fit in the pot.

Secure the lid and set the Pressure Release to **Sealing**. Select the **Steam** setting and set the cooking time for 0 (zero) minutes at low pressure. (The pot will take about 10 minutes to come up to pressure, which will be enough time for the chard to wilt.)

While the chard is cooking, working in two or three batches, depending on the size of your food processor, add the mushrooms to the processor and pulse about five times, until finely chopped. Transfer to a large bowl. Cut the onion and chard stems into 1-inch pieces, then combine them in the food processor and pulse about five times, until finely chopped. Transfer to the bowl with the mushrooms. Fit the food processor with the shredding disk, then shred the zucchini and transfer to the bowl. Then, shred the carrots and transfer to the bowl. (Alternatively, you can finely chop the mushrooms, chard stems, and onions with a knife, and grate the zucchini and carrots on the large holes of a box grater.)

When the cooking program ends, perform a quick pressure release by moving the Pressure Release to **Venting**. Open the pot and, and wearing heat-resistant mitts, grab the handles of the steam rack, lift out the rack, and set it on a plate. Lift out the inner pot, discard the water, and return the inner pot to the housing.

Press the **Cancel** button to reset the cooking program. Then select the **Sauté** setting and add the oil, salt, pepper, and finely chopped vegetables, setting the large bowl aside. Cook for 15 minutes, stirring occasionally, until most of the liquid released by the vegetables evaporates and the vegetables have cooked down quite a bit. Wearing heat-resistant mitts, lift out the inner pot. Press the **Cancel** button to reset the cooking program. Stir the rice and tomato paste into the vegetables, then transfer back to the bowl.

Rinse out the inner pot, then return it to the housing. Pour in 1½ cups water. Have ready the double-stacked stainless-steel pans.

Lay a chard leaf, veiny-side up, on a clean work surface, with the wide end nearest you. Scoop ¼ cup of the vegetable and rice mixture onto the wide end, fold in both sides of the leaf toward the filling, then roll up the leaf, enclosing the filling completely. Set the stuffed leaf, seam-side down, in one of the pans. Repeat with the remaining chard leaves and vegetable mixture, using the second pan when the first one is full. You may have extra vegetables; leave them in the bowl.

To make the sauce: Add the tomato sauce, water, vinegar, Worcestershire, and sugar to the bowl with any remaining vegetables and stir to combine.

Ladle half the sauce over the stuffed rolls in each pan. Stack the pans, cover with their lid, and secure the metal sling around the pans. Holding the handles of the sling, lower the stack into the Instant Pot.

Secure the lid and set the Pressure Release to **Sealing**. Select the **Manual** or **Pressure Cook** setting and set the cooking time for 30 minutes at high pressure. (The pot will take about 15 minutes to come up to pressure before the cooking program begins.)

When the cooking program ends, let the pressure release naturally for 10 minutes, then move the Pressure Release to **Venting** to release the remaining steam. Open the pot and, wearing heat-resistant mitts, use the sling's handle to lift the stacked pans out of the pot. Unclasp the sling and unstack the pans, being careful not to get burned by the steam.

Using a flexible spatula, transfer two or three rolls to each individual plate. Serve immediately.

NOTE

Chard leaves and other cooking greens vary widely in size. For this recipe, use small to medium leaves, with the leaf portions measuring about 8 inches long. If your chard leaves are very large, cut them in half crosswise before steaming. If you like, use collard greens instead of chard.

Quinoa and Sweet Potato Bowls with Cilantro Lime Vinaigrette

SERVES 6

2 cups quinoa, rinsed and drained

2½ cups low-sodium vegetable broth (page 152)

2 pounds (about 6) small sweet potatoes, 1½ to 2 inches in diameter

VINAIGRETTE

⅓ cup fresh lime juice (from 3 limes)

⅓ cup avocado oil or grapeseed oil

1 teaspoon agave nectar

½ teaspoon fine sea salt

¼ teaspoon freshly ground black pepper

¼ teaspoon ground cumin

1½ tablespoons chopped fresh cilantro

½ small red cabbage (12 ounces), shredded

1 orange or yellow bell pepper, seeded and sliced into thin strips

2 Roma or plum tomatoes, cored and diced

3 medium or 6 tiny avocados, sliced

Smoky Tomato Aioli (page 118), Chipotle Cashew Cream (page 157), or hot sauce for drizzling

Putting together a grain bowl is even easier when you can cook two of the ingredients in the Instant Pot at the same time. Here, sweet potatoes steam on a tall rack over the quinoa below. Crunchy raw vegetables and a fresh, citrus-based vinaigrette brighten up the bowl. It's especially important to seek out small, single-serving sweet potatoes for this recipe, since larger ones won't cook through by the time the quinoa is done.

———————

Add the quinoa and broth to the Instant Pot and stir to combine. Place a tall steam rack in the pot, making sure all of its legs rest firmly on the bottom of the pot. Place the sweet potatoes in a single layer on the rack.

Secure the lid and set the Pressure Release to **Sealing**. Select the **Manual** or **Pressure Cook** setting and set the cooking time for 10 minutes at low pressure. (The pot will take about 15 minutes to come up to pressure before the cooking program begins.)

While the sweet potatoes and quinoa are cooking, make the vinaigrette: In a tightly lidded jar, combine the lime juice, oil, agave, salt, pepper, cumin, and cilantro. Shake to combine. Set aside.

When the cooking program ends, let the pressure release naturally for 5 minutes, then move the Pressure Release to **Venting** to release any remaining steam. Open the pot and, using tongs, transfer the sweet potatoes to a dish. Wearing heat-resistant mitts, remove the rack, then lift out the inner pot. Use a fork to fluff the quinoa. Slice the sweet potatoes into ½-inch rounds.

In a large bowl, combine the cabbage, bell pepper, and tomatoes, and pour in the vinaigrette. Toss to combine.

Divide the quinoa and cabbage mixtures evenly among serving bowls. Arrange the sweet potato rounds on top, along with the sliced avocado. Drizzle with smoky tomato aioli, chipotle cashew cream, or hot sauce, and serve warm.

Gado Gado Salad with Lemongrass Tempeh

Don't be fooled by the word "salad" in this recipe title—it's actually a hearty Indonesian-meets–Sri Lankan feast. Steamed and raw vegetables are napped in a rich and spicy coconut-peanut sauce, and pan-fried tempeh is coated with a sweet lemongrass glaze. The tempeh is inspired by a dish called Tempeh La La from Malabar in Santa Cruz, California, a gem of a Sri Lankan restaurant where I ate at least once a month during my college years.

———————

To make the salad: Add 1 cup water to the Instant Pot and place a wire mesh steamer basket inside. Add the potatoes, carrots, and green beans to the steamer basket.

Secure the lid and set the Pressure Release to **Sealing**. Select the **Steam** setting and set the time for 2 minutes at low pressure. (The pot will take about 10 minutes to come up to pressure before the cooking program begins.)

While the vegetables are steaming, make the sauce: In a widemouthed mason jar, combine the coconut milk, peanut butter, brown rice syrup, lime juice, sambal, salt, and garlic. Use an immersion blender to blend for about 1 minute, until smooth.

When the cooking program ends, perform a quick pressure release by moving the Pressure Release to **Venting**. Open the pot and use a pair of tongs to transfer the vegetables to a dish to cool.

continued

SERVES 4

SALAD

12 ounces (10–12) fingerling or creamer potatoes, halved lengthwise

8 ounces (4 medium) carrots, peeled and cut into 3-inch sticks

8 ounces green beans, stem ends trimmed

6 cocktail-sized tomatoes, halved

1 English cucumber, sliced

PEANUT SAUCE

½ cup coconut milk

⅓ cup smooth natural peanut butter

2 tablespoons brown rice syrup or agave nectar

1 tablespoon fresh lime juice

2 teaspoons sambal oelek

1 clove garlic, minced

½ teaspoon fine sea salt

Gado Gado Salad with Lemongrass Tempeh, continued

TEMPEH

6 tablespoons avocado oil or other neutral oil

1 (12-ounce) package tempeh, cut into ¼ by 2-inch slices

4 cloves garlic, minced

2 teaspoons sambal oelek

1 tablespoon seedless tamarind paste, broken up in 1 cup water

2 stalks lemongrass, outer leaves removed, bottom 8 inches cut into 2-inch lengths, and bruised

¼ cup turbinado or organic cane sugar

2 tablespoons fried shallots (see page 161)

¼ cup chopped peanuts

Steamed rice (page 146) for serving

NOTE

If you do not already have cooked rice on hand, you can cook it in the Instant Pot according to the instructions on page 146, after steaming the vegetables, while you are preparing the tempeh in a skillet on the stove.

While the vegetables are cooling, make the tempeh: In a large nonstick skillet, heat 4 tablespoons of the oil over medium heat for about 3 minutes, until the oil is shimmering but not smoking. Add half of the tempeh and sear for about 8 minutes, turning once halfway through, until it is light golden brown. Transfer the tempeh to a paper towel–lined plate. Add the remaining 2 tablespoons oil to the skillet. Repeat the searing step with the remaining half of the tempeh and transfer it to the plate.

Add the garlic to the skillet and sauté for about 30 seconds, just until it begins to brown. Add the sambal, tamarind mixture, lemongrass, and sugar. Simmer for 10 to 12 minutes, until most of the water has evaporated and you have a reduced, syrupy sauce. Remove the lemongrass. Return the tempeh to the skillet and toss with the sauce until evenly coated. Turn off the heat. Sprinkle the fried shallots on top of the tempeh.

To serve, arrange the steamed vegetables on serving plates, along with the tomatoes and cucumber. Spoon a generous amount of peanut sauce over the vegetables, and top with chopped peanuts. Serve the tempeh and rice alongside.

Seitan Stroganoff

Strips of seitan lend just the right chewy texture to this stroganoff, so nobody will ever miss the meat. Stirred in at the last minute, a homemade vegan sour cream adds creaminess and tang. Stroganoff is total comfort food, and if you've made the seitan and soaked your cashews in advance, it only takes about a half hour to make. Alternatively, you can use store-bought seitan and sour cream if you want to skip the advance prep.

Select the high **Sauté** setting on the Instant Pot, add the oil, and heat for 1 minute. Add the garlic, shallots, mushrooms, and salt and sauté for 5 minutes, until the shallots soften and the mushrooms begin to wilt and give up their liquid. Add the seitan and sauté for about 2 minutes more, just to warm through. Stir in the tomato paste, mustard, Worcestershire, thyme, pepper, broth, and pasta, using a wooden spoon to nudge most of the pasta into the liquid; it's okay if a few pieces are sticking out a little bit, but try to get them in as flat a layer as possible.

Secure the lid and set the Pressure Release to **Sealing**. Press the **Cancel** button to reset the cooking program. Then select the **Manual** or **Pressure Cook** setting and set the cooking time for 6 minutes at high pressure. (The pot will take about 10 minutes to come up to pressure before the cooking program begins.)

When the cooking program ends, let the pressure release naturally for 5 minutes, then move the Pressure Release to **Venting** to release any remaining steam. Open the pot and stir in the sour cream. Taste and adjust the seasoning with salt, if needed.

Spoon the stroganoff into bowls and sprinkle with the parsley. Serve piping hot.

SERVES 6

1 tablespoon extra-virgin olive oil

2 cloves garlic, minced

3 large shallots (6 ounces), diced

8 ounces shiitake caps or cremini mushrooms, or a mix of both, thinly sliced

½ teaspoon fine sea salt, plus more as needed

8 ounces seitan (half recipe, page 151), sliced ¼-inch thick

1 tablespoon tomato paste

1 tablespoon Dijon mustard

1 tablespoon vegan Worcestershire sauce

½ teaspoon dried thyme

½ teaspoon freshly ground black pepper

3 cups low-sodium vegetable broth (page 152)

12 ounces rotini pasta

1 cup vegan sour cream (page 157)

1 tablespoon chopped fresh flat-leaf parsley

CHAPTER 6

Vegetable Sides

Spicy Ratatouille

SERVES 6

1 (1-pound) globe eggplant, cut into 1-inch pieces

3 zucchini, cut into 1-inch pieces

1 teaspoon fine sea salt

2 tablespoons extra-virgin olive oil, plus more for serving

1 large yellow onion, cut into 1-inch pieces

2 cloves garlic, minced

1 teaspoon dried basil

½ teaspoon freshly ground black pepper

½ teaspoon dried thyme

½ teaspoon red pepper flakes

1 bay leaf

3 yellow, orange, or red bell peppers, stemmed, seeded, and cut into 1-inch pieces

1 (14½-ounce) can diced tomatoes

¼ cup dry white wine or low-sodium vegetable broth (page 152)

Fresh basil leaves for serving

Crusty bread for serving

My favorite way to serve ratatouille is with big slices of crusty bread, either as-is if the bread is super fresh, or toasted, rubbed with garlic, and drizzled with olive oil if it needs a little refresh. That way you get to eat the soft, herbed vegetables, then soak up all of their delicious cooking liquid with the bread. Ratatouille is also good over rice or pasta, and I sometimes use the leftovers as a pizza topping.

———————

In a large bowl, toss together the eggplant and zucchini with the salt. Let stand for 15 minutes.

Select the **Sauté** setting on the Instant Pot, add the oil, and heat for 1 minute. Add the onion and garlic and sauté for about 4 minutes, until the onion softens. Add the basil, black pepper, thyme, red pepper flakes, and bay leaf and sauté for about 1 minute. Add the eggplant-zucchini mixture and any liquid that has pooled in the bottom of the bowl, along with the bell peppers, tomatoes and their liquid, and wine. Stir to combine.

Secure the lid and set the Pressure Release to **Sealing**. Press the **Cancel** button to reset the cooking program. Then select the **Manual** or **Pressure Cook** setting and set the cooking time for 2 minutes at low pressure. (The pot will take about 15 minutes to come up to pressure before the cooking program begins.)

When the cooking program ends, perform a quick pressure release by moving the Pressure Release to **Venting**. Open the pot and discard the bay leaf. Spoon the ratatouille into a serving bowl.

Drizzle the ratatouille with oil and sprinkle with fresh basil. Serve warm, with crusty bread.

NOTE

If you love your spice, feel free to increase the amount of red pepper flakes to your taste.

Beet Salad with Avocado, Orange, and Almond Feta

A bright and fresh beet salad is always a hit, especially when topped with dollops of creamy, tangy almond feta. Unlike some vegan cheese recipes, this one is easy with no presoaking required. The feta recipe makes enough to use half for this salad and half for Greek-Style Lima Beans (page 53).

To make the salad: Pour 1 cup water into the Instant Pot and place the wire metal steam rack in the pot. Arrange the beets in a single layer on the steam rack.

Secure the lid and set the Pressure Release to **Sealing**. Select the **Steam** setting and set the cooking time for 20 minutes at high pressure. (The pot will take about 10 minutes to come up to pressure before the cooking program begins.)

While the beets are cooking, prepare an ice bath.

To make the vinaigrette: In a widemouthed 1-pint jar, combine the oil, lemon juice, oregano, salt, pepper, and garlic. Using an immersion blender, blend until an emulsified vinaigrette forms. Set aside.

When the cooking program ends, perform a quick pressure release by moving the Pressure Release to **Venting**. Open the pot and, using tongs, transfer the beets to the ice bath and let cool for 10 minutes. (If you haven't done so already, you can use this time to prep the oranges and avocado.)

Using a paring knife, remove the skins from the beets; they should peel off very easily. Trim and discard the ends of the beets, then slice them into wedges.

In a large bowl, toss the spinach with half of the vinaigrette. Arrange the spinach on a large serving plate or on individual salad plates, then top with the beets, oranges, avocado, and mint. Using a pair of spoons, scoop bite-sized pieces of the feta out of its container and dollop it onto the salad. Spoon the rest of the vinaigrette over the salad and serve immediately.

continued

SERVES 4

SALAD

1 pound (about 4 medium) beets, each about 2½ inches in diameter

2 navel oranges, peeled and cut into segments

1 large or 4 small avocados, pitted, peeled, and sliced

1 (5- to 6-ounce) bag baby spinach

4 sprigs fresh mint, leaves removed and torn if large

¾ cup Almond Feta (recipe follows)

VINAIGRETTE

¼ cup extra-virgin olive oil

2 tablespoons fresh lemon juice

½ teaspoon dried oregano

¼ teaspoon fine sea salt

¼ teaspoon freshly ground black pepper

1 clove garlic, minced

Beet Salad with Avocado, Orange, and Almond Feta, continued

ALMOND FETA

MAKES ABOUT 1½ CUPS

1¼ cups (5 ounces) slivered or whole blanched almonds

¼ cup fresh lemon juice

¼ cup extra-virgin olive oil

2 tablespoons water

1 teaspoon nutritional yeast

1 teaspoon fine sea salt

NOTES

For a more crumbly feta, spread it out on a paper towel in a ¼-inch layer, place another towel on top, and press firmly to wick out the excess moisture. Scrape the feta off of the paper towel and break it into small crumbles.

In a food processor, combine the almonds, lemon juice, oil, water, nutritional yeast, and salt. Process for 30 seconds, scrape down the sides of the processor, then process for 1 minute more, until the mixture is mostly smooth (it will still have a bit of texture from the almonds). Transfer the feta to an airtight container, packing it down and spreading it out in an even layer. It will keep, refrigerated, for up to 1 week.

Patatas Bravas with Smoky Tomato Aioli

SERVES 4

1½ pounds (about 2) extra-large russet potatoes, scrubbed clean and cut into 1-inch cubes

2 tablespoons extra-virgin olive oil

½ teaspoon fine sea salt

½ cup Smoky Tomato Aioli (recipe follows)

2 tablespoons chopped fresh flat-leaf parsley

2 green onions, white and tender green parts, thinly sliced

This dish is inspired by a little dive bar in San Francisco that served a fried potato dish. They called it "Papas Fritas," but it was more like Spanish *patatas bravas* on steroids. This vegan version harks back to Spain with a smoked paprika–tinged aioli, but the copious toppings give it a fresh, modern flair.

———————

Preheat the oven to 425°F. Line a rimmed baking sheet with a silicone baking mat or aluminum foil.

Pour 1 cup water into the Instant Pot. Place a wire metal steam rack in the pot and add the potatoes.

Secure the lid and set the Pressure Release to **Sealing**. Select the **Steam** setting and set the cooking time for 2 minutes at high pressure. (The pot will take about 10 minutes to come up to pressure before the cooking program begins.)

When the cooking program ends, perform a quick pressure release by moving the Pressure Release to **Venting**. Open the pot and use tongs to remove the potatoes and arrange them in a single layer on the prepared baking sheet. Drizzle the oil over the potatoes, then sprinkle them evenly with the salt.

Bake the potatoes for about 25 minutes, until golden brown and crispy.

Transfer the potatoes to a serving dish. Drizzle with the aioli and sprinkle on the parsley and green onions. Serve hot.

continued

Patatas Bravas with Smoky Tomato Aioli, continued

SMOKY TOMATO AIOLI

MAKES 1¼ CUPS

¼ cup water

¼ cup avocado oil or grapeseed oil

2 tablespoons apple cider vinegar

1 teaspoon soy sauce, tamari,
or coconut aminos

¼ cup raw cashews, soaked in water
for 2 hours at room temperature,
or up to overnight in the refrigerator,
and drained

1 clove garlic, minced

1½ teaspoons tomato paste

1½ teaspoons nutritional yeast

¾ teaspoon smoked paprika

¼ teaspoon fine sea salt

In a widemouthed 1-pint jar, combine the water, oil, vinegar, soy sauce, cashews, garlic, tomato paste, nutritional yeast, smoked paprika, and salt in the order listed. Using an immersion blender, blend until thick and smooth, about 1 minute. Store, refrigerated, for up to 1 week. The liquid may begin to separate after a few days. If this happens, stir to recombine before using.

Carrot and Parsnip Coins with Tahini Sauce

Sweet carrots, earthy parsnips, and lemony tahini sauce make a great side dish or topping for a grain or salad bowl. Serve them with Winter Tabbouleh (page 37) for a Mediterranean-inspired meal.

To make the carrots and parsnips: Pour 1 cup water into the Instant Pot. Add the parsnips and carrots to a wire-mesh steamer basket, with the parsnips on the bottom and the carrots on top.

Secure the lid and set the Pressure Release to **Sealing**. Select the **Steam** setting and set the cooking time for 1 minute at low pressure. (It will take about 15 minutes to come up to pressure before the cooking program begins.)

While the vegetables are cooking, make the tahini sauce: In a widemouthed mason jar, combine the tahini, water, oil, lemon juice, salt, cumin, and garlic. Using an immersion blender, blend for about 30 seconds, until smooth. Stir in a teaspoon or two of additional water for a thinner sauce, if needed. Taste for seasoning, adding more salt, if needed. The tahini sauce can be stored in a tightly lidded container, refrigerated, for up to 1 week.

When the cooking program ends, perform a quick pressure release by moving the Pressure Release to **Venting**. Wearing heat-resistant mitts, lift out the steamer basket of carrots and parsnips. Lift out the inner pot and pour out the water.

Transfer the carrots and parsnips to the inner pot (you do not need to return it to the housing). Add the oil, parsley, and salt, and toss to combine.

Transfer the seasoned vegetables to a serving dish. Drizzle with ⅓ cup of the tahini sauce. Sprinkle za'atar on top and serve warm or at room temperature.

SERVES 8

CARROTS AND PARSNIPS

1 pound (4 medium) parsnips, cut into ¼-inch coins

1 pound (8 medium) carrots, cut into ¼-inch coins

1½ tablespoons extra-virgin olive oil

1 tablespoon chopped fresh flat-leaf parsley

½ teaspoon fine sea salt

TAHINI SAUCE

¼ cup tahini

¼ cup water, plus more as needed

2 tablespoons extra-virgin olive oil

2 tablespoons fresh lemon juice

¼ teaspoon fine sea salt, plus more as needed

⅛ teaspoon ground cumin

1 clove garlic, minced

1 teaspoon za'atar

NOTE

You can store leftover tahini sauce and use as a sandwich spread, a dip for crudités, or a condiment for pita pockets.

Eggplant Adobo

1 (1-pound) eggplant, cut into 1-inch pieces

1 teaspoon fine sea salt

¼ cup low-sodium soy sauce

2 tablespoons palm vinegar or coconut vinegar

2 tablespoons avocado oil or other neutral oil

4 cloves garlic, minced

1 large shallot, diced

1 red bell pepper, seeded and cut into 1-inch squares

½ teaspoon freshly ground black pepper

2 tablespoons water

Hot steamed rice (page 146) for serving

1 green onion, tender green part only, thinly sliced

NOTES

Salting the eggplant makes it cook up tender and silky, and helps it to give off enough liquid for the pot to come up to pressure. Using low-sodium soy sauce keeps this dish from getting too salty.

Use palm or coconut vinegar if you can find it (most Asian grocery stores have them). If you're unable to find either of those, substitute white vinegar or rice vinegar.

This adobo packs a tangy, salty punch. You'll definitely want to serve it over rice to offset the soy and vinegar sauce. You can cook up a pot of rice while you salt the eggplant and prep the other ingredients, then cook the adobo, which takes about 15 minutes start to finish. Definitely don't skip the salting step— it helps to make the eggplant nice and tender without using lots of oil.

———————

In a colander, toss the eggplant with the salt. Let sit in the sink or on top of a dish for 30 minutes (some liquid will release from the eggplant as it sits), then rinse the eggplant well under running water. Pat the pieces dry with paper towels.

In a small bowl, combine the soy sauce and vinegar. Set aside.

Select the **Sauté** setting on the Instant Pot, add the oil, and heat for 1 minute. Add the garlic and shallot and sauté for 3 minutes, until the shallot softens and the garlic begins to color. Add the eggplant, bell pepper, and black pepper, and stir to coat the vegetables with the oil (this will also help to unstick any browned bits from the bottom of the pot).

Pour in the vinegar mixture and water. Secure the lid and set the Pressure Release to **Sealing**. Press the **Cancel** button to reset the cooking program. Then select the **Manual** or **Pressure Cook** setting and set the cooking time for 2 minutes at low pressure. (It will take about 5 minutes for the pot to come up to pressure before the cooking program begins.)

When the cooking program ends, perform a quick release by moving the Pressure Release to **Venting**. Open the pot and give the vegetables a gentle stir to coat with the sauce, then let sit for a minute or two.

Spoon over bowls of steamed rice and sprinkle green onions on top. Serve hot.

Smoky Collard Greens and Carrots

The hint of smoke in these collards and carrots comes from one of my favorite ingredients, smoked paprika. It's one of those spices that, when used judiciously, adds a background note that's sometimes hard to achieve in vegan cooking, especially without lighting a grill. Serve these as a side dish for Hoppin' John Burgers (page 95) for a Southern-inspired meal.

———————————

Select the **Sauté** setting on the Instant Pot, add the oil, and heat for 1 minute. Add the onion and carrots and sauté for about 4 minutes, until the onion begins to soften. Stir in the collards and sauté for about 2 minutes, until wilted. Stir in the smoked paprika, salt, pepper, and water. Dollop the tomato paste on top, but do not stir it in.

Secure the lid and set the Pressure Release to **Sealing**. Press the **Cancel** button to reset the cooking program. Then select the **Manual** or **Pressure Cook** setting and set the cooking time for 5 minutes at high pressure. (The pot will take about 10 minutes to come up to pressure before the cooking program begins.)

When the cooking program ends, perform a quick pressure release by moving the Pressure Release to **Venting**. Open the pot and stir to incorporate the tomato paste. Taste and adjust the seasoning with salt, if needed.

Spoon the collards into a serving bowl or onto serving plates. Serve warm.

SERVES 4 TO 6

1 tablespoon extra-virgin olive oil

1 yellow onion, diced

8 ounces (4 medium) carrots, peeled and diced

2 bunches (about 1 pound) collard greens, stems discarded and leaves sliced into 1-inch ribbons

½ teaspoon smoked paprika

½ teaspoon fine sea salt, plus more as needed

¼ teaspoon freshly ground black pepper

½ cup water

1 tablespoon tomato paste

Succotash

I just love a vegetable side dish made entirely from ingredients in my pantry and freezer, don't you? Succotash is a summer treat you can have any time of the year. Even better, corn kernels and baby lima beans go into the pot straight from the freezer, no thawing required.

——————————

Select the **Sauté** setting on the Instant Pot, add the oil and garlic, and heat for 2 minutes, until the garlic is bubbling but not browned. Add the onion and sauté for about 5 minutes, until the onion softens. Add the lima beans, corn, tomatoes and their liquid, broth, thyme, salt, and pepper, and vegetable broth. Stir to combine.

Secure the lid and set the Pressure Release to **Sealing**. Press the **Cancel** button to reset the cooking program. Then select the **Manual** or **Pressure Cook** setting and set the cooking time for 3 minutes at high pressure. (The pot will take about 15 minutes to come up to pressure before the cooking program begins.)

When the cooking program ends, perform a quick pressure release by moving the Pressure Release to **Venting**. Open the pot and stir the succotash, then transfer to a serving bowl. Serve warm.

SERVES 6 TO 8

2 tablespoons extra-virgin olive oil

1 clove garlic, minced

1 yellow onion, diced

1 (16-ounce) bag frozen baby lima beans

1 (12-ounce) bag frozen corn kernels

1 (14½-ounce) can diced tomatoes

½ cup low-sodium vegetable broth (page 152)

½ teaspoon dried thyme

½ teaspoon fine sea salt

¼ teaspoon freshly ground black pepper

"Sour Cream" Mashed Potatoes

SERVES 4

1½ pounds (2 extra-large or 3 large) russet potatoes, peeled and sliced into ¾-inch rounds

½ cup unsweetened nondairy milk

½ cup vegan sour cream, homemade (page 157) or store-bought

¾ teaspoon fine sea salt, plus more as needed

¼ teaspoon freshly ground black pepper, plus more as needed

NOTE

For a twist on this traditional mash, substitute 2 parsnips, peeled and sliced into ¾-inch rounds, for 8 ounces of the potatoes.

Creamy, well-seasoned mashed potatoes are easy to love. They're a versatile side dish for holidays or anytime, and vegan sour cream adds just the right amount of richness. I make them most often when I'm pan-frying or oven-roasting something else—the Instant Pot is the perfect place to keep the potatoes warm until everything is ready to serve.

———————————

Pour 1 cup water into the Instant Pot and place a steamer basket in the pot. Add the potatoes to the basket.

Secure the lid and set the Pressure Release to **Sealing**. Select the **Steam** setting and set the cooking time for 4 minutes at high pressure. (The pot will take about 10 minutes to come up to pressure before the cooking program begins.)

When the cooking program ends, perform a quick pressure release by moving the Pressure Release to **Venting**. Open the pot and, wearing heat-resistant mitts, lift out the steamer basket. Lift out the inner pot and discard the water.

Return the potatoes to the still-warm inner pot. Add the nondairy milk, sour cream, salt, and pepper, then use a potato masher to mash the potatoes to your desired texture. Taste for seasoning and add more salt and pepper, if needed.

Spoon the mashed potatoes into a serving bowl and serve warm.

Maple Mashed Sweet Potato Casserole

Be the Thanksgiving MVP and bring this beautiful side dish of sweet potatoes covered in golden browned marshmallows. You'll make the mashed sweet potatoes in the Instant Pot (and at that point you can serve them as is if you want), then top them with marshmallows (see Notes for vegan sources) and bake 'til golden brown. Just like Mom used to make!

Pour 1 cup water into the Instant Pot and place a steamer basket in the pot. Add the sweet potatoes to the basket.

Secure the lid and set the Pressure Release to **Sealing**. Select the **Steam** setting and set the cooking time for 5 minutes at high pressure. (The pot will take about 15 minutes to come up to pressure before the cooking program begins.)

While the sweet potatoes are steaming, preheat the oven to 325°F. Grease a 2-quart baking dish with coconut oil and line a baking sheet with aluminum foil.

When the cooking program ends, perform a quick pressure release by moving the Pressure Release to **Venting**. Open the pot and, wearing heat-resistant mitts, lift out the steamer basket. Lift out the inner pot and discard the water.

Return sweet the potatoes to the still-warm inner pot. Add the coconut oil, maple syrup, salt, and cinnamon, then use a potato masher to mash the sweet potatoes until smooth.

Spoon the mashed potatoes into the baking dish. Top with a single layer of the marshmallows, cut side down. Place the dish on the prepared baking sheet. Bake for 25 to 30 minutes, until the marshmallows are puffed and golden brown on top. Serve warm.

SERVES 6 TO 8

3 pounds (about 4) large sweet potatoes, peeled and cut into 1-inch pieces

¼ cup coconut oil

¼ cup dark maple syrup

1 teaspoon fine sea salt

½ teaspoon ground cinnamon

10 vegan marshmallows (half of a 10-ounce bag), cut in half lengthwise

NOTES

Vegan marshmallows are getting easier and easier to find these days. I've seen them at Whole Foods, Trader Joe's, in other natural food stores, and on Amazon.

You can also serve the sweet potatoes straight from the Instant Pot, without the marshmallow topping. Top with chopped toasted pecans and lime zest.

This recipe is easily halved to serve a smaller group. The cooking time will remain the same. Do not reduce the amount of steaming water in the Instant Pot.

CHAPTER 7

Desserts and Beverages

Creamy Cardamom Rice Pudding

MAKES ABOUT
4 CUPS

½ cup long-grain, jasmine, or basmati rice

1½ cups water

1 (13½-ounce) can coconut milk

1 small (5¼-ounce) can coconut cream

½ cup brown rice syrup or agave nectar

½ teaspoon ground cardamom

¼ teaspoon fine sea salt

¼ cup currants

¼ cup chopped pistachios

Creamy and coconutty with a whiff of fragrant cardamom, this rice pudding takes flavor notes from Indian *kheer*. The preparation is all Instant Pot, though—it cooks in about 20 minutes, and most of that time is unattended. Chopped pistachios make a gorgeous topping, but you can also use toasted almonds, if you have those on hand.

———————

Combine the rice and water in the Instant Pot. Secure the lid and set the Pressure Release to **Sealing**. Select the **Manual** or **Pressure Cook** setting and set the cooking time for 5 minutes at high pressure. (The pot will take about 10 minutes to come up to pressure before the cooking program begins.)

While the rice is cooking, in a blender, combine the coconut milk, coconut cream, brown rice syrup, cardamom, and salt. Blend at medium speed for about 30 seconds, until smooth. Set aside.

When the cooking program ends, let the pressure release naturally for 10 minutes, then move the Pressure Release to **Venting** to release any remaining steam. Open the pot and use a whisk to break up the cooked rice. Whisking constantly, pour the coconut milk mixture in a thin stream into the rice.

Press the **Cancel** button to reset the cooking program. Then select the **Sauté** setting. Cook the pudding for about 5 minutes, whisking constantly, until it is thickened and bubbling.

The pudding will still be pourable at this point but will set as it cools. Press the **Cancel** button to turn off the pot. Wearing heat-resistant mitts, lift out the inner pot. Stir in the currants.

Pour the pudding into a glass or ceramic dish or into individual serving bowls. Cover and refrigerate the pudding for at least 4 hours, or up to overnight (it gets better the longer it chills).

Just before serving, sprinkle the pudding with chopped pistachios. Serve chilled.

Strawberry-Rhubarb Compote

There are classic pairings, and then there are perfect ones like strawberries and rhubarb. They're in season at the same time, and the sweetness of the berries combines with the tart, tangy rhubarb to make a well-balanced compote. Left to my own devices, I'd happily eat a bowl on its own, but for company I serve it over vanilla coconut ice cream.

——————————

Combine the rhubarb, strawberries, sugar, and cardamom in the Instant Pot and stir well, making sure to coat the rhubarb and strawberries evenly with the sugar. Let the mixture sit for 15 minutes, until the fruit releases its moisture. This is all of the liquid you will need for the recipe. Give the mixture another good stir.

Secure the lid and set the Pressure Release to **Sealing**. Select the **Manual** or **Pressure Cook** setting and set the cooking time for 5 minutes at low pressure. (The pot will take about 10 minutes to come up to pressure before the cooking program begins.)

Let the pressure release naturally (this will take about 15 minutes). When the pressure has fully released, open the pot and stir the compote to break down the rhubarb.

Transfer the compote to a heatproof container, where it will continue to thicken as it cools. Serve the compote warm or chilled. It will keep in the refrigerator for up to 1 week.

MAKES ABOUT
4 CUPS

1 pound rhubarb (about 4 large stalks), trimmed and cut into 1-inch pieces

1 pound strawberries, hulled and quartered lengthwise

½ cup turbinado or organic cane sugar

½ teaspoon ground cardamom

NOTE

To make this recipe in an 8-quart Instant Pot, double the quantities of all of the ingredients.

Lemon-Ginger Cheesecake with Speculoos Cookie Crust

SERVES 8

No-bake vegan cheesecakes abound, but this Instant Pot version is in a league of its own. Tofu and soaked cashews combine to make a dense and silky-smooth cheesecake filling flavored with lemon and ginger that sits atop a delicious spiced crust made of crushed speculoos cookies.

CRUST

14 speculoos cookies

1 tablespoon coconut oil, melted and cooled

FILLING

1 (14-ounce) block firm tofu, drained

1 cup raw cashews, soaked in water for 2 hours at room temperature, or up to overnight in the refrigerator, and drained

½ cup turbinado or organic cane sugar

Finely grated zest of 1 lemon

2 tablespoons fresh lemon juice

1 tablespoon arrowroot

1 teaspoon ground ginger

¼ teaspoon fine sea salt

¼ cup coconut oil, melted and cooled

2 tablespoons egg replacer powder

¼ cup water

Vegan whipped cream for serving

Sliced strawberries for serving

Line the base of a 7-inch round springform or push-up pan with an 8-inch round of parchment paper. If using a springform pan, secure the collar on the pan, closing it onto the base so that the parchment round is clamped in. Lightly grease the sides of the pan with oil or nonstick cooking spray.

To make the crust: In a food processor, process the cookies to fine crumbs. Add the coconut oil. Using 1-second pulses, process until the mixture resembles damp sand. Transfer the crumb mixture to the prepared pan and press firmly into an even layer on the bottom and about ½ inch up the sides of the pan. Place the pan in the freezer to allow the crust to firm up a bit while you make the filling. Wipe out the food processor.

To make the filling: Cut the tofu into 1-inch slices. Sandwich the slices in a single layer between double layers of paper towels or a folded kitchen towel, and press firmly to wick away as much moisture as possible. Break the slices into 1-inch pieces and add them to the food processor. Add the cashews, sugar, lemon zest and juice, arrowroot, ginger, and salt. Process at high speed for about 2 minutes, until smooth. Scrape down the sides of the bowl, add the coconut oil, egg replacer, and water and process for 2 minutes more, until smooth.

Spoon the filling into the prepared crust. Use a spatula to spread out the filling in an even layer, then tap the pan gently against the counter a few times to remove any air bubbles in the filling. Cover the pan tightly with aluminum foil, then place the pan on a long-handled silicone steam rack.

Pour 1½ cups water into the Instant Pot. Holding the handles of the steam rack, lower it into the pot.

Secure the lid and set the Pressure Release to **Sealing**. Select the **Cake, Pressure Cook**, or **Manual** setting and set the cooking time for 35 minutes at high pressure. (The pot will take about 10 minutes to come up to pressure before the cooking program begins.)

When the cooking program ends, let the pressure release naturally for 10 minutes, then move the Pressure Release to **Venting** to release any remaining steam. Open the pot and, wearing heat-resistant mitts, grab the handles of the steam rack, lift the pan out of the pot, and set the pan on a cooling rack. Remove the aluminum foil, taking care not to let any condensation that has settled on top of the aluminum foil drip onto the cake. If any liquid has pooled on top of the cake, use a paper towel to gently blot it dry.

Let the cheesecake cool on the rack for 1 hour, then transfer to the refrigerator to chill for at least 4 hours, or up to 24 hours.

Unmold the cake by removing the collar from the springform pan, or by pushing the cake bottom up through the push-up pan with a drinking glass or mug. Slide the cake off of the parchment and onto a cake plate.

Slice cheesecake into wedges and serve, garnished with a dollop of whipped cream and some sliced strawberries.

Chocolate–Peanut Butter Cheesecake

SERVES 8

CRUST

4 ounces vegan chocolate cookies (13 Jovial brand Crispy Cocoa cookies)

1 tablespoon coconut oil, melted and cooled

FILLING

3 tablespoons egg replacer powder

⅓ cup water

1 (14-ounce) block firm tofu, drained

½ cup smooth natural peanut butter

¼ cup coconut oil, melted and cooled

½ cup turbinado or organic cane sugar

¼ cup cocoa powder

1 teaspoon instant coffee crystals or espresso powder

½ teaspoon fine sea salt

Chocolate lovers rejoice—this is the vegan dessert to beat them all. Chocolate and peanut butter are blended into the filling, and a rich ganache gets poured on top. You'll need to track down some vegan chocolate cookies for the crust—I like the Crispy Cocoa cookies from Jovial brand, available at Whole Foods and other natural food stores.

Line the base of a 7-inch round springform or push-up pan with an 8-inch round of parchment paper. If using a springform pan, secure the collar on the pan, closing it onto the base so that the parchment round is clamped in. Lightly grease the sides of the pan with oil or nonstick cooking spray.

To make the crust: In a food processor, process the cookies to fine crumbs. Add the coconut oil. Using 1-second pulses, process until the mixture resembles damp sand. Transfer the crumb mixture to the prepared pan and press firmly into an even layer on the bottom and about ½ inch up the sides of the pan. Place the pan in the freezer to allow the crust to firm up a bit while you make the filling. Wipe out the food processor.

To make the filling: In a small bowl, stir together the egg replacer and water, using a spoon to mash any lumps of egg replacer against the side of the bowl. Set aside.

Break the tofu into 1-inch pieces and add them to the food processor. Add the peanut butter, coconut oil, sugar, cocoa powder, instant coffee, and salt and process for 1 minute. Scrape down the sides of the bowl, add the egg replacer mixture, and process for 1 minute more, until smooth.

Spoon the filling into the prepared crust. Use a spatula to spread out the filling in an even layer, then tap the pan gently against the counter a few times to remove any air bubbles in the filling. Cover the pan tightly with aluminum foil, then place the pan on a long-handled silicone steam rack.

continued

Chocolate–Peanut Butter Cheesecake, continued

GANACHE

1 tablespoon coconut oil

¼ cup chocolate chips

2 tablespoons smooth natural peanut butter

2 tablespoons unsweetened nondairy milk

¼ cup chopped roasted peanuts

Pour 1½ cups water into the Instant Pot. Holding the handles of the steam rack, lower it into the pot.

Secure the lid and set the Pressure Release to **Sealing**. Select the **Cake, Pressure Cook,** or **Manual** setting and set the cooking time for 40 minutes at high pressure. (The pot will take about 10 minutes to come up to pressure before the cooking program begins.)

When the cooking program ends, let the pressure release naturally for 10 minutes.

While the pressure is releasing, make the ganache: In a small saucepan over low heat, combine the coconut oil, chocolate chips, peanut butter, and nondairy milk. Stir constantly for 3 to 4 minutes, until glossy and smooth. Remove from the heat and set aside.

After the 10 minutes of timed release are up, move the Pressure Release to **Venting** to release any remaining steam. Open the pot and, wearing heat-resistant mitts, grab the handles of the steam rack, lift the pan out of the pot, and set the pan on a cooling rack. Remove the aluminum foil, taking care not to let any condensation that has settled on the aluminum foil drip onto the cake. If any liquid has pooled on top of the cake, use a paper towel to gently blot it dry.

Pour the ganache onto the cake, then spread it out in an even layer, stopping ¼ inch from the sides of the cake. Sprinkle the chopped peanuts evenly over the ganache while it is still warm. Let the cheesecake cool on the rack for 1 hour, then transfer to the refrigerator and chill for at least 12 hours, or up to 24 hours.

Unmold the cake by removing the collar from the springform pan, or by pushing the cake bottom up through the push-up pan with a drinking glass or mug. Slide the cake off of the parchment and onto a cake plate.

Slice the cheesecake into wedges and serve.

Apple-Pear Sauce

Pears add a little something special to applesauce. This recipe is basic and kid-friendly, but my adult taste buds love it, too. My favorite way to have it is chilled, with a generous sprinkle of cinnamon on top.

———————————

Combine all of the ingredients in the Instant Pot. Secure the lid and set the Pressure Release to **Sealing**. Select the **Steam** setting and set the cooking time for 4 minutes at low pressure. (The pot will take about 10 minutes to come up to pressure before the cooking program begins.)

Let the pressure release naturally (this will take about 15 minutes). When the pressure has fully released, open the pot.

For a chunky sauce, use a potato masher to break up the apples and pears. For a smooth puree, use an immersion blender to blend the sauce.

Serve immediately, or let cool, transfer to an airtight container, and refrigerate for up to 1 week.

MAKES ABOUT
3 CUPS

1 pound (2 large) firm but ripe Anjou pears, peeled, quartered, and cored

1 pound (2 large) Granny Smith apples, peeled, quartered, and cored

¼ cup apple juice or water

NOTES

To freeze, let cool to room temperature, then scoop ½-cup portions into the wells of a silicone muffin pan and slip the pan into the freezer. When the portions have frozen solid, about 4 hours, pop them out of the muffin pan, put in ziplock plastic freezer bags, and return to the freezer. Store for up to 6 months.

To make this recipe in an 8-quart Instant Pot, double the quantities of all of the ingredients.

Dark and Fudgy Walnut Brownie Sundaes with Coconut Caramel Sauce

SERVES 8

3 tablespoons egg replacer powder

6 tablespoons water

¾ cup vegan shortening, melted and cooled (I recommend Nutiva or Earth Balance brand)

1½ teaspoons instant coffee crystals or espresso powder

1½ teaspoons vanilla extract

1 cup turbinado or organic cane sugar

½ teaspoon fine sea salt

¼ cup unsweetened nondairy milk

¾ cup all-purpose flour

¾ cup cocoa powder

¾ cup chocolate chips

¾ cup walnut halves and pieces, toasted

NOTE

The caramel sauce takes just under 3 hours to make, including cooling time in the Instant Pot. You can make it while the brownies are cooling, as directed, or make it ahead of time.

Brownies turn out moist and fudgy when you make them in the Instant Pot because the steam keeps them from drying out. They'll emerge from the pot looking kind of jiggly and strange, but have some faith and patience—after they've cooled for a couple hours, they set beautifully. Slice the brownies into wedges (they cook in a circular cake pan) and serve them with big scoops of vegan ice cream, then, for the pièce de résistance, top them with the easiest caramel sauce you'll ever make.

———————

Line the base of a 7-inch round springform or push-up pan with an 8-inch round of parchment paper. If using a springform pan, secure the collar on the pan, closing it onto the base so that the parchment round is clamped in. Lightly grease the sides of the pan with oil or nonstick cooking spray.

In a small bowl, stir together the egg replacer and water, using a spoon to mash any lumps of egg replacer against the side of the bowl. Set aside.

In a mixing bowl, whisk together the shortening, instant coffee, vanilla, sugar, and salt. Whisk in the nondairy milk and egg replacer mixture. Stir in the flour and cocoa powder, just until the dry ingredients are incorporated. Fold in the chocolate chips and walnuts.

Transfer the batter to the prepared pan; it will be very thick. Use a spatula to pat it out into an even layer. Cover the pan tightly with aluminum foil, then place the pan on a long-handled silicone steam rack.

Pour 1½ cups water into the Instant Pot. Holding the handles of the steam rack, lower it into the pot.

Secure the lid and set the Pressure Release to **Sealing**. Select the **Cake, Pressure Cook,** or **Manual** setting and set the cooking time for 45 minutes at high pressure. (The pot will take about 10 minutes to come up to pressure before the cooking program begins.)

When the cooking program ends, let the pressure release naturally for 10 minutes, then move the Pressure Release to **Venting** to release any remaining steam. Open the pot and, wearing heat-resistant mitts, grab the handles of the steam rack, lift the rack out of the pot, and set the pan on a cooling rack. Remove the aluminum foil, taking care not to let any condensation that has settled on the aluminum foil drip onto the brownies.

Let the brownies cool for at least 2 hours, or up to 24 hours, before serving.

While the brownies are cooling, make the coconut caramel sauce: Pour 1 cup water into the Instant Pot and place a wire metal steam rack inside. Place the unopened can of sweetened condensed coconut milk in the center of the rack.

Secure the lid and set the Pressure Release to **Sealing**. Select the **Steam** setting and set the cooking time for 45 minutes, then deselect the **Keep Warm** setting so that the pot will turn off when the cooking program ends. (The pot will take about 5 minutes to come up to pressure before the cooking program begins.)

When the cooking program ends, leave the can in the pot to cool for 2 hours, undisturbed.

After 2 hours, open the pot and remove the can; it will still be a bit warm. You can use the caramel while it is still warm, or chill in the refrigerator for a few hours, where it will thicken a bit. After opening the can, transfer the caramel to an airtight container and store, refrigerated, for up to 1 month.

When the brownies are cool, slice them into wedges, transfer to serving plates, and serve with a scoop of ice cream and caramel sauce drizzled on top.

COCONUT CARAMEL SAUCE (MAKES ABOUT 1 CUP)

1 (11¼-ounce) can sweetened condensed coconut milk

Coconut vanilla ice cream for serving

Hibiscus-Agave Sippers

SERVES 8

1 loosely packed cup (1 ounce) dried hibiscus flowers

2 cinnamon sticks, broken in half

½ teaspoon whole allspice berries

8 cups water

16 teaspoons agave nectar, plus more to taste

NOTES

You can also serve this drink iced for a refreshing cooler. Substitute a 2-inch knob of ginger, cut into thin slices, for the allspice berries. Chill the drink, then serve it over ice, sweetened with agave.

Either the hot or chilled version of this drink can be spiked with rum.

Flor de Jamaica, or hibiscus flowers, are available in Mexican grocery stores and online. You can usually find them hanging in clear cellophane bags, near the dried peppers, cinnamon sticks, and spices. They don't look like much when they're dried, but when steeped, they unfurl and lend their beautiful magenta color to this aromatic tisane.

Place a wire-mesh steamer basket in the Instant Pot and add the hibiscus flowers, cinnamon sticks, and allspice berries to the basket. Pour in the water.

Secure the lid and set the Pressure Release to **Sealing**. Select the **Pressure Cook** or **Manual** setting and set the cooking time for 0 (zero) minutes at low pressure. (The pot will take about 20 minutes to come up to pressure before the cooking program begins.)

When the cooking program ends, let the pressure release for 10 minutes, then move the Pressure Release to **Venting** to release any remaining steam. (You can also let the pressure release naturally. The drink will get more strongly flavored the longer it steeps.)

Open the pot and, wearing heat-resistant mitts, lift out the steamer basket. Leave the drink on the **Keep Warm** setting until ready to serve, up to 10 hours.

Ladle the drink into mugs. Sweeten each mug with agave, starting with 2 teaspoons per cup and adding more to taste.

Peppermint Hot Chocolate

A thermos full of hot chocolate is the best winter accessory. Add peppermint for a bracing twist on the traditional, sub in vanilla to make a classic version, or add liqueur for a hot cocktail. Use any nondairy milk you like; just make sure it's unsweetened, or use a little less sugar in the hot chocolate if your milk does contain sweetener.

———————————

Combine the nondairy milk, cocoa powder, sugar, peppermint extract, and salt in the Instant Pot and whisk for 1 minute. Select the low **Sauté** setting and set the cooking time for 9 minutes. Cover the pot with the glass lid. After 4 minutes, open the pot, whisk the mixture for 1 minute, then cover with the lid again. When the timer goes off, give the hot chocolate a final whisk.

Ladle the hot chocolate into mugs and serve topped with marshmallows.

SERVES 4

4 cups unsweetened nondairy milk

¼ cup cocoa powder

6 tablespoons turbinado or organic cane sugar

¾ teaspoon peppermint extract

¼ teaspoon fine sea salt

Vegan marshmallows for serving (optional; see Notes on page 125)

NOTES

For a traditionally flavored hot chocolate, substitute vanilla extract for the peppermint extract.

For a hot cocktail, substitute ½ cup of peppermint liqueur (such as Peppermint Mocha Kahlúa) for the peppermint extract, reduce the amount of sugar to ¼ cup, and increase the cooking time to 10 minutes.

CHAPTER 8

Basics

Beans

MAKES ABOUT 6 CUPS

The Instant Pot makes it easy to prepare basic beans in advance, whether you like to soak them or not. Soaking does tend to produce more evenly cooked beans that hold their shape well, while lentils never require soaking. I like to use the Delay Start function for beans, letting them soak in salted water for 8 to 12 hours before the cooking program begins. Smaller beans such as black beans or pintos can soak for as little as 8 hours to become fully hydrated, while larger beans like chickpeas or *gigantes* beans take longer, at least 10 hours. Soak your beans for as long as is required for them to plump up and lose their wrinkly appearance, or up to 12 hours if you need to leave them longer.

1 pound dried beans (any variety)

8 cups water

2 teaspoons fine sea salt

———————

Add the beans, water, and salt to the Instant Pot and stir to dissolve the salt.

Secure the lid and set the Pressure Release to **Sealing**. If soaking the beans, select the **Manual, Pressure Cook,** or **Bean/Chili** setting, then refer to the soaked cooking time in the table on the opposite page for setting the cooking time; use high pressure. Next, select the **Timer** or **Delay** function and set the time delay for at least 8 and up to 12 hours. (When the soaking time is complete, the pot will take about 20 minutes to come up to pressure before the cooking program begins.)

If you are cooking the beans right away, select the **Manual, Pressure Cook,** or **Bean/Chili** setting, then refer to the unsoaked cooking time in the table on the opposite page for setting the cooking time; use high pressure. (The pot will take about 20 minutes to come up to pressure before the cooking program begins.)

When the cooking program ends, let the pressure release naturally; this will take about 30 minutes. Open the pot and, wearing heat-resistant mitts, lift out the inner pot. If using the beans immediately, drain them in a colander. To refrigerate, ladle the beans and their cooking liquid into airtight containers, let cool for about 1 hour; then cover and refrigerate for up to 5 days. To freeze, drain the beans in a colander, portion them into 1-quart ziplock plastic freezer bags, seal well, and freeze for up to 6 months.

Lentils

MAKES ABOUT 6 CUPS

Lentils are a little trickier to pressure cook—they can often become mushy, with a fall-apart texture (which actually works well in soups and stews). Beluga and French green (Puy) lentil varieties are the best candidates for salads, since they hold their shape best, especially when cooked in small (1½-cup or less) batches with the pot-in-pot method.

1 cup lentils (any variety)

1½ cups water

½ teaspoon fine sea salt

———————

In a 1½-quart stainless-steel bowl, stir together the lentils, 1½ cups of the water, and the salt.

Pour 2 cups of water into the Instant Pot and place the wire metal steam or a tall steam rack in the pot. Put the bowl on the steam rack. Select the **Pressure Cook** or **Manual** setting and set the cooking time for 15 minutes at high pressure for firm lentils, or 20 minutes at high pressure for softer lentils. (It will take about 10 minutes for the pot to come to pressure before the cooking program begins.)

When the cooking program ends, you can perform a quick release by moving the Pressure Release to **Venting** or you can let the pressure release naturally. Open the pot and, wearing heat-resistant mitts, remove the bowl of lentils from the Instant Pot.

If any liquid remains in the bowl with the lentils, drain the lentils into a colander. Transfer the lentils to an airtight container, let cool for about 1 hour, then cover and refrigerate for up to 5 days. To freeze, transfer the lentils to a 1-quart ziplock plastic freezer bag, seal well, and freeze for up to 6 months.

TIME CHARTS FOR BEANS AND LENTILS

Beans	Soaked, Cooking Time (in minutes)	Unsoaked, Cooking Time (in minutes)
Black	10–15	20–25
Black-eyed pea	10–15	20–25
Cannellini	20–25	35–40
Chickpea (garbanzo bean)	20–25	35–40
Corona, giant lima, gigantes	20–25	25–30
Flageolet	10–15	20–25
Great Northern	20–25	25–30
Kidney	20–25	25–30
Lima	10–15	20–25
Navy	20–25	25–30
Pinquito	10–15	20–25
Pinto or Peruano	20–25	25–30
Red	10–15	20–25

Lentils	Unsoaked, Cooking Time (in minutes)
Beluga (black)	15 to 20
Green	15 to 20
Puy (French green)	15 to 20
Red (split)	15 to 18
Small brown (Spanish)	15 to 20
Yellow	15 to 18

Steamed Rice

1 CUP DRY RICE MAKES 3 CUPS COOKED

Whether you're using rice as the base of a grain bowl, in a wrap or burrito, or as an accompaniment to a main dish, the easiest way to prepare it is in the Instant Pot. You can set it and walk away, and there's no difficult rule to remember—you can always use a 1:1 ratio of rice to liquid. Whether you're cooking brown, white, long-grain, or short-grain rice, that ratio works perfectly. It results in firm-textured, separate grains, so if you like your rice to have a softer consistency, use a bit more liquid. (When making risotto, see page 36; you'll use even more liquid to achieve a looser consistency.)

Measure the rice into a wire-mesh strainer, then rinse under running water for 10 seconds, swishing the grains around. Set the strainer over a bowl and let the rice drain well, which should take about 1 minute. Remove the inner pot from the Instant Pot housing and pour the rice and an equal volume of water or broth into the inner pot. Jiggle the pot back and forth on the countertop so the rice settles in an even layer, then return the inner pot to the housing. Secure the lid and set the Pressure Release to **Sealing**.

For white rice, select the **Rice** setting. The pot will adjust the cooking time automatically. For brown rice, select the **Multigrain** setting and set the cooking time for 25 minutes.

When the cooking program ends, leave on the **Keep Warm** setting for 10 minutes, then move the Pressure Release to **Venting** to release any remaining steam. Open the pot and, wearing heat-resistant mitts, lift out the inner pot. Use a rice paddle to scoop the rice out of the pot. Serve warm or freeze for later use.

To freeze individual portions of rice, spread the hot rice in a thin layer on a rimmed baking sheet and let cool for about 20 minutes, until room temperature. Scoop the cooled rice into small plastic bags in single or double portions and seal closed. Slip the bags into 1-quart or 1-gallon ziplock plastic freezer bags, seal them closed, and freeze them flat. Rice will keep in the freezer for up to 2 months. When you're ready to eat the rice, transfer it, still frozen, to a bowl, cover the bowl with a reusable silicone lid or plastic wrap, and heat in the microwave for 2 to 3 minutes, until piping hot.

RULES FOR PERFECT RICE

- Because it's difficult to cook small amounts of rice evenly, use at least 1 cup in the 3-quart pot, 1½ cups in the 6-quart pot, or 2 cups in the 8-quart pot.

- To cook a smaller amount of rice, use the pot-in-pot method explained on page 9 and used in Jackfruit and Black Bean Burritos on page 97.

- Rinse your rice before cooking. In a wire-mesh strainer, swish it around under running water to rinse off any extra starch, then drain well. This step ensures that you won't end up with gummy, goopy rice, and the grains will come out separate and fluffy.

- Don't fill the pot more than half full of liquid. Grains and beans can foam and spatter when they cook. Keeping the pot no more than half-full prevents clogging the pressure valve.

- Letting the rice rest on the **Keep Warm** setting for 10 minutes once it finishes cooking ensures that the grains are evenly cooked and the moisture redistributes, with no sticking or burning on the bottom of the pot.

Whole Grains

You can cook any type of whole grain in the Instant Pot. While pearl barley, kasha, and quinoa are not technically whole grains, the cooking method is the same, so they are found in the table that follows.

For less than 1½ cups of uncooked grain, use the grain-to-water ratio, cooking time, and pressure indicated in the table below and cook according to the pot-in-pot method.

For 1½ cups or more of uncooked grain, combine the grain and water in the Instant Pot. Season with salt (optional).

Secure the lid and set the Pressure Release to **Sealing**, then refer to the table at left for setting the cooking time and pressure.

When the cooking program ends, let the pressure release naturally for 10 minutes, then move the Pressure Release to **Venting** to release any remaining steam. Open the pot and fluff the grains with a fork, if desired.

Serve or use immediately, or let cool to room temperature (to cool the grains quickly, spread them on a rimmed baking sheet), then transfer to an airtight container and refrigerate for up to 4 days or freeze for up to 2 months.

RULES FOR PERFECT WHOLE GRAINS

- Use the **Multigrain** setting when cooking 1½ cups or more; for smaller amounts, use the **Steam** setting and the pot-in-pot (PIP) method (see page 9).

- As with cooking rice, after adding the grain and water to the pot, make sure the pot is no more than half-full to prevent excessive foaming and/or bubbling and blocking of the mechanisms in the lid.

- If the grain-to-water ratio in the table contains a range for the amount of water, use the lesser amount if you like your grains with firmer texture; use the greater amount if you prefer them softer and more tender.

- The shorter cooking time will result in firmer grains, while the longer cooking time will result in softer grains.

COOKING WHOLE GRAINS

Grain	Grain: Water Ratio	Cooking Time (in minutes)	Pressure
Barley, pearl	1: 1½ to 2	25 to 30	High
Barley, pot	1: 3 to 4	25 to 30	High
Brown rice (short-, medium-, or long-grain)	1:1 to 1¼	20 to 25	High
Bulgur, coarse	1: 1½	10 to 15	Low
Freekeh, cracked	1: 1½	10 to 15	Low
Kasha (roasted buckwheat)	1: 1½	10 to 15	Low
Millet	1: 1⅔	10 to 12	High
Oats, steel-cut	1:3	25 to 30	High
Oats, whole groats	1:3	15 to 20	High
Quinoa, rinsed and drained	1:1¼ to 1½	12 to 15	Low
Wheat berries, rye berries, spelt, farro, and kamut	1: 1½ to 2	25 to 30	High
Wild rice	1: 1⅓ to 1½	25 to 30	High

Steamed Butternut or Spaghetti Squash

MAKES ABOUT 5 CUPS

Use cooked butternut squash, mashed with maple syrup and vegan butter, as a sweet side dish, stir it into oatmeal, or use it in recipes that call for canned pumpkin. Serve spaghetti squash as a light side dish tossed with olive oil, salt, and pepper, or serve it as you would pasta, with meatballs and arrabbiata sauce (page 41). Minimal prep is required to cook winter squash in the Instant Pot—simply quarter the squash, remove the seeds, then steam the pieces under pressure.

1 butternut or spaghetti squash,
no larger than 3½ pounds

Pour 1½ cups water into the Instant Pot. Place the wire metal steam rack in the pot.

Trim off the stem end of the squash, cut the squash lengthwise into quarters, and scoop out and discard the seeds. Place the squash quarters on the steam rack in the pot, arranging the pieces in a single layer.

Secure the lid and set the Pressure Release to **Sealing**. Select the **Steam** setting and set the cooking time for 7 minutes at high pressure. (The pot will take about 10 minutes to come up to pressure before the cooking program begins.)

When the cooking program ends, perform a quick pressure release by moving the Pressure Release to **Venting**. Open the pot and, using tongs, transfer the squash to a plate or cutting board. Set aside until cool enough to handle, about 5 minutes. Use a spoon to scoop the flesh from the skin of the butternut squash, or a fork to separate the strands of the spaghetti squash. Discard the skin.

Use immediately, or let cool to room temperature, transfer to an airtight container, and refrigerate for up to 3 days. The texture of spaghetti squash tends to suffer when frozen, while pureed butternut squash freezes well, for up to 3 months.

Seitan

MAKES ABOUT 1 POUND

1 cup vital wheat gluten

2 tablespoons nutritional yeast

½ teaspoon granulated garlic

½ teaspoon fine sea salt

¼ teaspoon freshly ground black pepper

2 cups low-sodium vegetable broth (page 152)

In a mixing bowl, combine the wheat gluten, nutritional yeast, garlic, salt, and pepper. Add ¾ cup of the broth and stir until a ball of dough forms and comes away from the sides of the bowl. Add another tablespoon or two of broth if all of the dry ingredients are not fully absorbed. Turn the dough out onto a board and knead for about 2 minutes, until a cohesive, very springy dough forms.

Roll the dough into a 6-inch log. Slice the log into 1-inch rounds, then slice each round into five to six 1-inch pieces.

Arrange the pieces of seitan dough in the Instant Pot in an even layer, letting them touch as little as possible. Pour the remaining 1¼ cups broth into the pot, pouring it over the pieces of dough. It will not quite cover the pieces completely.

Secure the lid and set the Pressure Release to **Sealing**. Press the **Cancel** button to reset the cooking program. Then select the **Manual** or **Pressure Cook** setting and set the cooking time for 15 minutes at high pressure. (The pot will take about 10 minutes to come up to pressure before the cooking program begins.)

When the cooking program ends, perform a quick pressure release by moving the Pressure Release to **Venting**. Open the pot and use a slotted spoon to transfer the pieces of seitan to a dish. Use right away, or let the seitan cool to room temperature, then transfer to a tightly lidded container, pour the cooking liquid over the top, and store in the refrigerator for up to 1 week.

Low-Sodium Vegetable Broth

MAKES ABOUT 2 QUARTS

This broth contains a fairly low level of sodium. It is comparable to store-bought low-sodium vegetable broth, low-sodium bouillon, and reduced-sodium Better Than Bouillon. If you use a full-sodium, store-bought broth in the recipes in this book, you may need to reduce the amount of salt and/or other salty ingredients.

1 tablespoon extra-virgin olive oil

1 large yellow onion, diced

4 cloves garlic, smashed

2 large carrots, diced

4 celery stalks, diced

2 teaspoons fine sea salt

2 tablespoons tomato paste

2 tablespoons nutritional yeast

8 cups water

1 teaspoon black peppercorns

2 bay leaves

1 (3-ounce) bunch flat-leaf parsley

———————

Select the **Sauté** setting on the Instant Pot, add the oil, and heat for 1 minute. Add the onion, garlic, carrots, celery, and salt. Sauté for about 10 minutes, until the vegetables give up some of their liquid and begin to brown just a bit. Stir in the tomato paste and nutritional yeast, then add 1 cup of the water and use a wooden spoon to nudge loose any browned bits

from the bottom of the pot. Add the peppercorns, bay leaves, parsley, and remaining 7 cups water, making sure not to fill the pot more than two-thirds full.

Secure the lid and set the Pressure Release to **Sealing**. Press the **Cancel** button to reset the cooking program. Then select the **Soup/Broth** setting and set the cooking time for 10 minutes at high pressure. (The pot will take about 20 minutes to come up to pressure before the cooking program begins.)

Place a wire-mesh strainer over a large stainless-steel bowl. For a clearer broth, line the strainer with a double layer of cheesecloth.

When the cooking program ends, let the pressure release naturally for 30 minutes, then move the Pressure Release to **Venting** to release any remaining steam. Open the pot and, wearing heat-resistant mitts, lift out the inner pot and pour the broth through the prepared strainer into the bowl. Discard the vegetables. Let the broth cool to room temperature. (To speed the cooling process, set the bowl in a larger bowl containing an ice bath.)

The broth can be used right away, stored in an airtight container in the refrigerator for up to 3 days, or frozen for up to 6 months.

Mushroom Broth

MAKES ABOUT 2½ QUARTS

1 ounce dried shiitake mushrooms, stems removed

1 ounce mixed dried mushrooms

2 teaspoons fine sea salt

1 teaspoon black peppercorns

1 bay leaf

10 cups water

_____

Combine all the mushrooms, the salt, peppercorns, bay leaf, and water in the Instant Pot.

Secure the lid and set the Pressure Release to **Sealing**. Select the **Soup/Broth** setting and set the cooking time for 10 minutes at high pressure. (The pot will take about 25 minutes to come up to pressure before the cooking program begins.)

When the cooking program ends, let the pressure release naturally for 45 minutes, then move the Pressure Release to **Venting** to release any remaining steam. Open the pot and, using a slotted spoon, remove the mushrooms; if you like, save them for another use, such as adding to Hot and Sour Soup (page 74) or another soup or stew.

Set a wire-mesh strainer over a large stainless-steel bowl and line the strainer with a double layer of cheesecloth.

Wearing heat-resistant mitts, lift out the inner pot and pour the broth through the prepared strainer into the bowl. Discard the solids in the strainer. Let the broth cool to room temperature. (To speed the cooling process, set the bowl in a larger bowl containing an ice bath.)

The broth can be used right away, stored in an airtight container in the refrigerator for up to 3 days, or frozen for up to 6 months.

Steamed Potatoes and Vegetables

The method for steaming any vegetable is the same.

Since potatoes can vary so much in diameter, their cooking time varies as well. To account for this, the cooking time recommendations for whole potatoes are given in ranges.

You can also steam potatoes quartered, sliced, or cubed. The 6-quart Instant Pot can hold a maximum of 4 pounds of potatoes, but I find that I get the most even and consistent results when I steam 3 pounds or less.

Pour 1 cup water into the Instant Pot. If cooking whole potatoes or large vegetables, place the wire metal steam rack in the pot; if cooking small or chopped/sliced potatoes or vegetables, place a steamer basket in the pot. Add the potatoes or vegetables to the pot.

Secure the lid and set the Pressure Release to **Sealing**. Select the **Steam** setting, then refer to the time charts on these pages for setting the cooking time; use high pressure for potatoes and winter squash, and low pressure for other vegetables. (Depending on the quantity of vegetables, the pot will take 10 to 20 minutes to come up to pressure before the cooking program begins.)

When the cooking program ends, perform a quick pressure release by moving the Pressure Release to **Venting**. Open the pot and use tongs to remove whole potatoes or vegetables, or wear heat-resistant mitts to lift out the steamer basket or steam rack.

Serve immediately, or let cool to room temperature, transfer to an airtight container, and refrigerate for up to 3 days.

TIME CHART FOR POTATOES

Whole Potatoes (Regular and Sweet)	Cooking Time (in minutes, at high pressure)
Baby/Creamer (1 to 2 ounces)	5
Small (3 to 4 ounces)	8 to 10
Medium (5 to 7 ounces)	10 to 12
Large (8 to 10 ounces)	12 to 15
Extra Large (11 to 13 ounces)	20 to 25
Jumbo (14 to 16 ounces)	28 to 30
Prepared Potatoes (Regular and Sweet)	**Cooking Time (in minutes, at high pressure)**
Quartered (medium)	5
Sliced (½ to ¾ inch thick)	3 to 4
Cubed (1 inch)	3

TIME CHART FOR VEGETABLES

Vegetables	Fresh, Cooking Time (in minutes)	Frozen, Cooking Time (in minutes)
Artichokes, medium to jumbo	10 to 15	n/a
Artichokes, hearts	4 to 5	5 to 6
Asparagus	1 to 2	2 to 3
Beets, small, whole	11 to 13	13 to 15
Beets, large, whole	20 to 25	25 to 30
Broccoli, florets	1 to 2	3 to 4
Broccoli, stalks	2 to 3	4 to 5
Brussels sprouts, whole	2 to 3	4 to 5
Cabbage, red, purple, or green, shredded	1 to 2	3 to 4
Carrots, sliced	1 to 2	2 to 3
Carrots, whole or chunks	2 to 3	3 to 4
Cauliflower florets	1 to 2	3 to 4
Celery, chunks	1 to 2	3 to 4
Corn, kernels	1 to 2	2 to 3
Corn, on the cob	2 to 3	4 to 5
Eggplant, slices or chunks	2 to 3	3 to 4
Endives, whole	1 to 2	2 to 3
Escarole, chopped	1 to 2	2 to 3
Green beans, whole	2 to 4	4 to 6
Greens (beet greens, collards, kale, Swiss chard, turnip greens)	3 to 6	4 to 7

Vegetables	Fresh, Cooking Time (in minutes)	Frozen, Cooking Time (in minutes)
Leeks, chopped	2 to 4	3 to 5
Mixed vegetables, chopped	2 to 3	3 to 4
Okra, sliced	1 to 2	2 to 3
Onions, sliced	2 to 3	3 to 4
Parsnips, sliced	1 to 2	2 to 3
Peas, sugar snap or snow, whole	1 to 2	2 to 3
Peas, green (English), shelled	1 to 2	2 to 3
Pumpkin, small slices or chunks	4 to 5	6 to 7
Pumpkin, large slices or chunks	8 to 10	10 to 14
Spinach	1 to 2	3 to 4
Squash, acorn, slices or chunks	6 to 7	8 to 9
Squash, butternut, slices or chunks	8 to 10	10 to 12
Sweet peppers, slices or chunks	1 to 3	2 to 4
Tomatoes, quartered	2 to 3	4 to 5
Tomatoes, whole	3 to 5	5 to 7
Turnips, chunks	2 to 4	4 to 6
Zucchini, slices or chunks	1 to 2	3 to 4

Roasted Garlic

MAKES 2 BULBS

2 bulbs garlic, left whole

2 teaspoons extra-virgin olive oil

¼ teaspoon fine sea salt

———————

Pour 1 cup water into the Instant Pot and place the wire metal steam rack inside.

Cut off the top ½ inch of the garlic bulbs, exposing the cloves. Place the bulbs cut-side-up on the steam rack.

Secure the lid and set the Pressure Release to **Sealing**. Select the **Steam** setting and set the cooking time for 10 minutes at high pressure. (The pot will take about 5 minutes to come up to pressure before the cooking program begins.)

While the garlic is steaming, preheat the oven or toaster oven to 425°F and line a baking sheet with foil.

When the cooking program ends, perform a quick pressure release by moving the Pressure Release to **Venting**. Open the pot and use a pair of tongs to transfer the garlic to the prepared baking sheet.

Drizzle the oil over the garlic, then sprinkle with salt. Bake for 12 to 15 minutes, until golden brown.

Let the bulbs cool for about 10 minutes, until you can handle them comfortably. Holding a bulb upside down, squeeze the base of each clove so that the cloves slide out of their skins. Repeat with the remaining bulb.

Use the garlic right away or store in a tightly lidded container, refrigerated, for up to 3 days, or frozen, for up to 12 months.

Caramelized Onions

MAKES ABOUT 2½ CUPS

The salt is important in this recipe, so don't omit it. It helps the onions give up their liquid so they cook down properly and caramelize.

¼ cup avocado oil or other neutral oil

2 pounds (4 large) yellow onions, halved and sliced ¼ inch thick

1 teaspoon fine sea salt

———————

Select the High **Sauté** setting on the Instant Pot (the timer will default to 30 minutes), add the oil, and heat for 1 minute. Add the onions and salt and stir with a wooden spoon, separating the onion layers and coating the slices with the oil. Cover the pot with the glass lid and let the onions sweat, without stirring, for 10 minutes.

Uncover the pot and, wearing a heat-resistant mitt, hold the rim of the inner pot in place while you stir the onions vigorously, using the spoon to nudge loose any browned bits from the bottom of the pot. Leave the pot uncovered and set a timer for 4 minutes. Stir the onions vigorously again, making sure to nudge loose any browned bits. Set the timer for 3 minutes, then stir the onions vigorously again and continue to stir them at 2-minute intervals until the 30-minute **Sauté** cooking program has ended. Wearing heat-resistant mitts, lift out the inner pot.

The onions can be used right away, stored in an airtight container in the refrigerator for up to 4 days, or frozen for up to 3 months.

To freeze the onions, let cool to room temperature, then scoop ½-cup portions into the wells of a silicone muffin pan and slip the pan into the freezer. When the portions have frozen solid, about 4 hours, pop them out of the muffin pan, put in ziplock freezer bags, and return to the freezer.

Chipotle Cashew Cream

MAKES 1¾ CUPS

½ cup raw cashews, soaked in water
for 2 hours at room temperature,
or up to overnight in the refrigerator,
and drained

½ cup water

½ cup avocado oil or grapeseed oil

2 tablespoons fresh lime juice

2 cloves garlic, peeled

1 canned chipotle in adobo sauce

2 tablespoons nutritional yeast

2 teaspoons chili powder

1 teaspoon fine sea salt

————————

In a blender, combine all of the ingredients. Blend at high speed until creamy and smooth, about 1 minute.

Store leftovers, refrigerated, for up to 1 week. If you see some liquid separating out, stir to recombine. Chipotle cashew cream doubles as a killer substitute for nacho cheese.

Vegan Sour Cream

MAKES 1 CUP

½ cup raw cashews, soaked in water
for 2 hours at room temperature,
or up to overnight in the refrigerator,
and drained

¼ cup avocado oil or grapeseed oil

2 tablespoons water

2 tablespoons fresh lemon juice

1 tablespoon nutritional yeast

½ teaspoon fine sea salt

————————

In a widemouthed pint jar, combine the cashews with the oil, water, lemon juice, nutritional yeast, and salt. Using an immersion blender, blend the mixture until smooth, about 2 minutes. Store in a tightly lidded container, refrigerated, for up to 1 week.

GRAIN AND SALAD BOWLS

Grain and salad bowls are popping up at so many fast-casual restaurants for a reason—they're one of the best ways to create a vibrant, nutritious, all-in-one meal. You can prep them in advance, pack them for lunch, or have them ready for dinner after a busy day.

To build a bowl, you'll want to have a variety of raw and cooked ingredients, with complementary flavors and contrasting textures. Pick and choose from the categories here, and try to include at least one item from each category for a balanced bowl.

Greens, Grains, or Both

Start with your base. For a lighter meal, choose salad greens such as romaine, arugula, or spring mix. For a bowl with more staying power, go for cooked grains like quinoa, brown rice, or cracked wheat. If you can't decide, have both. Refer to pages 146 and 148 for instructions and cooking times for rice and whole grains.

Raw and Cooked Vegetables

A mix of raw and cooked vegetables is my favorite way to go. Raw vegetables can be anything you'd put in a salad, such as crunchy julienned carrots or sliced snap peas; for cooked vegetables, choose steamed and chilled broccoli, green beans, or whatever your favorites are. Refer to pages 154–55 for instructions and cooking times for vegetables.

Proteins and Good Fats

Incorporate some filling ingredients into your bowl. Proteins can be simple options like cooked beans or lentils (pages 144–45), or cubed and seared tofu (follow instructions for searing from Palak Tofu, page 88, and season with salt and pepper). You can also choose something with lots of flavor, like garlic sausages (page 80) or lemongrass tempeh (page 107).

Good fats really help to round out a bowl, too. A few slices of ripe avocado, spoonfuls of almond feta (page 115), or a handful of toasted nuts or seeds are some of my favorites. You can also drizzle in a flavorful oil, such as extra-virgin olive oil, walnut oil, or pumpkinseed oil.

Dressings and Sauces

There are lots of vinaigrettes, dressings, and sauces in this book that would be welcome additions to a grain or salad bowl. Drizzle on some cilantro lime vinaigrette (page 104), french vinaigrette (page 61), tahini sauce (page 119), peanut sauce (page 107), Smoky Tomato Aioli (page 118), or Chipotle Cashew Cream (page 157). If you want to go really basic, just use oil, vinegar, salt, and pepper.

Prepping Your Bowls

Once you've decided what to put in your bowl, all that's left is to round up the ingredients and prepare as many servings of each component as you'll need. I usually make 6 to 8 servings at a time—I'll have a bowl for lunch on Sunday, then have the rest on hand for the week ahead. Store separate ingredients in mason jars or stackable, lidded containers to save on fridge space, keep the dressing or sauce stored separately, then add everything to a big bowl when you're ready to serve.

THE CRUNCH FACTOR: TOPPINGS FOR INSTANT POT MEALS

The only downfall of pressure cooking is its inability to create crispy, crunchy results straight out of the pot. After all, for the pressure to build, you need steam, and for steam, you need liquid (at least a cup or so in a 6-quart Instant Pot). You can certainly sear or broil foods after cooking (as with Cassoulet with Garlic Sausages, page 80, or Mac 'n' Trees, page 45), and a topping of herbed bread crumbs doesn't hurt either.

An even easier option is to keep crispy, crunchy toppings on hand to liven up your pressure-cooked meals. Here are some of my favorites.

Nuts and Seeds

I always throw some toasted nuts on my oatmeal—try chopped peanuts on top of Steel-Cut PBJ Oatmeal (page 25), or toasted almonds on a bowl of more simply cooked old-fashioned oats (page 26). Sunflower seeds and toasted walnuts are my go-tos for grain bowls (page 158). Chopped pistachios add crunch and gorgeous color to rice pudding (page 128).

Chips, Crackers, and Croutons

Fritos or other corn chips on Winter Vegetable Chili (page 84) is one of my favorite combinations. Earth Balance makes Vegan Cheddar Flavor Squares—crumble those on Mac 'n' Trees (page 45) for a no-bake, crunchy topping. And, of course, some potato chips never go amiss tucked into a chickpea salad sandwich (page 100). The artichoke (page 68) and split pea soups (page 79) in this book are topped with homemade croutons, which are easy and always worth toasting up.

Fresh Fruits and Vegetables

Don't underestimate the power of raw produce to liven up a cooked meal. A few slices of crisp apple or radish, julienned bell peppers or carrots, or some fresh chopped onion are some of my go-tos.

Store-Bought Crispy Bits

Fried shallots and fried garlic are available in jars at most Asian grocery stores, and they're good on just about anything. They are usually unseasoned, so their neutral flavor goes with every cuisine.

Another option are bacon (flavored) bits, which, as it turns out, are more often than not vegan products. Frontier Bac'uns, McCormick Bac'n Pieces, or some pan-fried Lightlife Fakin' Bacon add crunch as well as savory, smoky flavor.

FREEZING AND REHEATING: BROTHS, GRAINS, BEANS, AND LEFTOVERS

Whenever you're freezing something, it's useful to think about how convenient it will be to defrost later. Chances are, if it's in a big ol' hunk, you'll dread dredging it up from the depths of your freezer. If you've taken care to freeze small or individual servings, they'll be much easier to thaw.

Broths

To freeze: Place a silicone muffin pan or mini loaf pan on top of a baking sheet. Ladle the broth into the pan in ½-cup or 1-cup portions. Let it cool to room temperature, then pop it in the freezer until solid, at least 4 hours. At this point, you can easily unmold the frozen broth and transfer it to freezer bags, where it will stay good for up to 6 months.

To thaw: Place the frozen broth in a single layer in the Instant Pot. Select the **Manual** or **Pressure Cook** setting and set the cooking time for 5 minutes at high pressure. When the cooking program ends, perform a quick or natural pressure release.

Grains and Beans

To freeze: Spread out cooked grains or beans on a baking sheet and let them cool to room temperature. Scoop into sandwich or quart-sized freezer bags, press out most of the air, and seal them closed. Stack the bags flat in the freezer for space-saving storage, where the grains will stay good for up to 2 months.

To thaw: Break up the frozen grains or beans into 1- to 2-inch pieces, and put them in a 1½-quart stainless-steel bowl. Place the bowl on top of a steam rack in the Instant Pot, with a cup of water in the pot. Select the **Manual** or **Pressure Cook** setting and set the cooking time for 5 minutes at high pressure. When the cooking program ends, perform a quick or natural pressure release.

Leftovers

To freeze: This method works best for soups, stews, chilis, and other semiliquid leftovers. Place a silicone muffin pan or mini loaf pan on top of a baking sheet. Spoon the leftovers into the pan in ½-cup or 1-cup portions. Let it cool to room temperature, then pop it in the freezer until solid, at least 4 hours. At this point, you can easily unmold the frozen leftovers and transfer them to freezer bags, where they will stay good for up to 6 months.

To thaw: Place up to four ½-cup portions or two 1-cup portions in a single layer in a 1½-quart stainless-steel bowl. Place the bowl on top of a steam rack in the Instant Pot, with a cup of water in the pot. Select the **Manual** or **Pressure Cook** setting and set the cooking time for 5 minutes at high pressure. When the cooking program ends, perform a quick or natural pressure release.

Resources

Here are a few of my favorite brands for products used in the recipes in this book.

Aroy-D (curry pastes, coconut milk) thai-united.com/en/aroy-d (purchase online at Amazon)

Banyan Botanicals (yellow lentils, also called moong/mung dal) banyanbotanicals.com

Better Than Bouillon (reduced-sodium vegetable base) betterthanbouillon.com

Bob's Red Mill (oatmeal, kasha, flageolet and other beans, nutritional yeast, egg replacer powder, xanthan gum, arrowroot starch) bobsredmill.com

Earth Balance (vegan buttery spread, baking sticks) earthbalancenatural.com

Edward & Sons (bouillon cubes, vegan Worcestershire sauce, panko bread crumbs) store.edwardandsons.com

Jovial (crispy cocoa cookies) jovialfoods.com

Native Forest (coconut cream) store.edwardandsons.com

Nature's Charm (sweetened condensed coconut milk) naturescharmveganproducts.com

Nutiva (shortening, coconut oil, chia seeds) nutiva.com

Oaktown Spice Shop (ras el hanout) oaktownspiceshop.com

Trader Joe's (canned jackfruit, speculoos cookies) traderjoes.com

Wholesome Sweeteners (turbinado sugar) wholesomesweet.com

Acknowledgments

Ever since my undergraduate days of Vegan Wednesday potlucks at the University of California, Santa Cruz, music building, I've wanted to write a vegan cookbook. More than a decade later, and with the help and support of many, here it is in all of its vegetable-filled glory.

It's been especially fun tasking my vegetarian (and vegetable-loving) friends with recipe testing. Thanks so much to Lindsey McLennan Burdick and Nick Burdick, Lizzie Paulsen and Norman Kuo, Katie Vroom, Nancy Tariga, Jenny Hong, and my parents, Cindy and Larry Harris.

To my agent, Alison Fargis, thank you for helping to make this happen. I am so happy to have you on my team. To my editor, Lisa Westmoreland, project editor, Shannon Welch, and everyone at Ten Speed Press, I am honored to be writing for a publishing house made up of so many talented people. To Kara Plikaitis, Colin Price, Ryan Reineck, and Ellen Ottman, thank you for art directing, shooting, and styling this book so beautifully.

To Robert Wang, Anna Di Meglio, and everybody at Double Insight (aka Instant Pot headquarters), thanks for manufacturing the appliance that started this electric pressure cooking revolution. The IP love is real!

To my husband, Brendan, thank you for taste-testing every single recipe in this book, and for being my rock amidst a year of big changes. I'm so happy to be at the beginning of our Pacific Northwest chapter with you.

Finally, to all of my cookbook-writing and blogging friends, thank you for your inspiration, mentorship, and generosity of spirit. We are all so lucky to be able to do what we love.

About the Author

Coco Morante is the author of the best-selling *Essential Instant Pot Cookbook* and *Ultimate Instant Pot Cookbook*. She is a recipe developer, facilitator of the Instant Pot Recipes Facebook page, and creator of the blog *Lefty Spoon*. Her recipes and writing are featured in numerous print and online publications, including Epicurious, Popsugar, Food Republic, TASTE, The Kitchn, Simply Recipes, and *Edible Silicon Valley*.

Coco lives in Portland, Oregon, with her husband, Brendan, and their beagle, Beagle Brendan.

Index

Library of Congress Cataloging-in-Publication Data
Names: Morante, Coco, author. | Price, Colin, 1982- photographer.
Title: The essential vegan Instant Pot : fresh and foolproof plant-based recipes
    for your electric pressure cooker / Coco Morante ; photography by Colin Price.
Description: First edition. | California : Ten Speed Press, 2019. | Includes
    bibliographical references and index. |
Identifiers: LCCN 2018043081 (print) | LCCN 2018044436 (ebook)
Subjects: LCSH: Pressure cooking. | Electric cooking. | Vegan cooking. |
    Cooking (Natural foods) | LCGFT: Cookbooks.
Classification: LCC TX840.S63 (ebook) | LCC TX840.S63 M67 2019 (print) |
    DDC 641.5/6362—dc23
LC record available at https://lccn.loc.gov/2018043081

Hardcover ISBN: 978-0-399-58298-1
eBook ISBN: 978-0-399-58299-8

Printed in China

Design by Debbie Berne
Food and prop styling by Ryan Reineck

10 9 8 7 6 5 4 3 2 1

First Edition